BUSINE

D0070155

Seven Deadly Sins of
GARDENING

and the vices and virtues of gardeners

Seven Deadly Sins of
GARDENING

and the vices and virtues of gardeners

Toby Musgrave

with Mike Calnan

THE NATIONAL TRUST

To Vibeke

For your constant encouragement, always wise council
and ceaseless patience. Tak min skat, min dejligt kone.

First published in the United Kingdom in 2006
by National Trust Books
151 Freston Road
London W10 6TH

An imprint of Anova Books Company Ltd

Copyright © National Trust 2006
Text © Toby Musgrave 2006

Photographs © NTPL / John Hammond

All rights reserved. No part of this publication may be reproduced, stored
in a retrieval system, or transmitted in any form or by any means electronic,
mechanical, photocopying, recording or otherwise, without the prior written
permission of the copyright owner.

ISBN-10 1905400462
ISBN-13 9781905400461

A CIP catalogue record for this book is available from the
British Library.

10 9 8 7 6 5 4 3 2 1

Printed and bound by MPG Books Ltd, Cornwall
Reproduction by Anorax Imaging Ltd, Leeds

This book can be ordered direct from the publisher at the website:
www.anovabooks.com, or try your local bookshop. Also available at
National Trust shops.

* All properties marked with an asterisk are National Trust properties.
For more information please visit www.nationaltrust.org.uk.

R0412250746

THE CHICAGO PUBLIC LIBRARY TW

Contents

Introduction 6

Greed 8
Generosity 26

Pride 40

Lust 56
Love 80

Wrath 100

Sloth 108
Zeal 124

Envy 140

Gluttony 152

Bibliography 162

Index 168

Acknowledgements 176

introduction

The genesis of this book came about as a result of a conversation Mike Calnan and I had, over a glass of wine, at the conclusion of a conference on garden history. We had been invited within the hallowed portals of Bristol University to address the subject of garden history in the public realm (rather than in the ivory towers of academia). Mike, there in his capacity as the National Trust's Head of Gardens and Parks, had discussed the need to make garden history more fun and relevant to visitors and I had spoken about the need to popularize and make garden history accessible through the media.

I think both of us were taken aback when the keynote speaker, a respected academic, butted into our conversation to inform us that he did not agree with a single word we had said and felt that making garden history popular was tantamount to debasing a respectable field of academic endeavour. The traditional story of garden-making has focused on chronological periods, garden forms and a few famous designers. The people who actually had the gardens made, and why they did, are often glaringly absent from the story. With another glass of wine in hand, I said that the National Trust gardens must be filled with great 'people stories' and Mike confessed how for a long time he had wanted to tell the many, often hilarious, anecdotal stories he had heard over the years about National Trust gardens, their former owners, designers and gardeners. *Seven Deadly Sins of Gardening* contains those stories, and our thanks must go to the academic-who-shall-remain-nameless for his unwitting motivation.

We all enjoy the slightly voyeuristic thrill of having a peek at how the 'other half' lived – indeed why else does the National Trust annually attract 11 million visitors to the 300 houses and gardens currently in its care? And at first glance it may seem ridiculous to suggest that the gardens in the National Trust's care have anything in common with yours or mine. But when you strip away the history, the styles, the plants and the money, you'll find that each and every National Trust garden was made by, or for, a person or a couple and, just like your garden and mine, these gardens were an expression of a particular person's taste and feelings – their 'self', no less.

The time span covered by this book is about half a millennium, but it swiftly became apparent that while garden fashions have changed down the centuries, people, essentially, haven't. Humanity has been, and continues to be, blown along by the same set of emotional frailties, desires, aims, aspirations, wants and needs that have driven garden-makers to expressions of lust, greed, generosity, pride, love, wrath, sloth, zeal, envy and gluttony.

Toby Musgrave and Mike Calnan

greed

'A longing to possess something.
Excessive consumption.'

We all have those moments of greed, of wanting to dash out and splash out on something special ... and expensive. Sometimes the call of a new sports car, a flashy piece of jewellery or an exotic holiday is just too loud to ignore and we return from our shopping frenzy with head held high; the proud new owner. But a garden cannot be gift-wrapped and carried home in triumph to be gloated over and, in some paradoxical way, greed in the form of garden-making (especially in the days before powered machinery) also taught patience. Nature cannot be hurried and there was (and is) no instant gratification. But that did not stop owners coveting the latest and most fashionable style, and paying a fortune for it. Even if, in many cases, it was their descendants who got to fully appreciate the results!

Attingham Park, *SHROPSHIRE* *
NOEL HILL, 1ST LORD BERWICK

To make a landscape in the centuries before powered machinery was a long, laborious and disruptive process. And as wealthy landowners demanded more privacy and bigger landscapes, so the social cost was sometimes paid by their tenants – poor farmers and agricultural workers. In many cases, those who had not been forced off the land by the Enclosure Acts of the 1760s now found their homes were considered a 'blot on the landscape' by the rich and powerful. To create the perfect vista, troublesome dwellings were simply flattened and the inhabitants forcibly relocated. Noel Hill, 1st Lord Berwick (1745–89)

as wealthy landowners demanded more privacy and bigger landscapes, so the social cost was sometimes paid by their tenants – poor farmers and agricultural workers

entirely swept away the mediaeval village of Berwick Maviston as part of landscape designer Thomas Leggett's improvements at Attingham Park in 1761–1772.

Castle Ward, *CO. DOWN* *
MAJOR ANDREW NUGENT

As late as the mid-19th century, Castle Ward was the venue for some rather questionable land clearance. When Major Andrew Nugent, second husband of Lady Bangor, wanted to enhance the much admired parkland and extend it over the Audleystown Peninsula, he cleared the small village of Audleystown in the process. The mainly Catholic residents were packed off to America and a rather picturesque bluebell wood was planted in their place.

Charlecote Park, *WARWICKSHIRE* *
GEORGE LUCY, 'CAPABILITY' BROWN

'Capability' Brown received a mere £561 from George Lucy (1714–86) for his work at Charlecote Park, which included moving two rivers – where legend has it that a young Will Shakespeare occasioned to poach deer. Perhaps Lucy bargained hard – certainly he was a somewhat eccentric character, fond of wearing an elaborately embroidered white satin suit. After a riotous time as a student he developed hypochondria and his behaviour became even stranger. After 'mending his health' in Portugal in 1755, he returned not with a straw donkey but a flock of Jacob sheep (whose descendants still roam the park today). Upon bumping into Lancelot 'Capability' Brown (1716–83) in Bath in April 1761, where Lucy was taking the waters for his health, Lucy told Brown that 'the time was elapsed for a second payment which he said was no matter as he did not want money, but upon my offering him a £100 note he pulled out his pocket book and carried it off with him'. Only the very rich can carry that much around in 'small change'!

Claremont Landscape Garden, *SURREY* *
CLIVE OF INDIA, 'CAPABILITY' BROWN

Even the equable Brown had his enemies and the contract to build 'the mansion … which, with the arrangement of the ground' at Claremont for Clive of India (1725–74) caused him a great deal of anguish. Sir William Chambers was so angry at being passed over for the job that he set about attacking Brown. His *Dissertation on Oriental Gardening* (1772) was a thinly veiled assault on the Brownian style and he even lowered himself to making offensive comments such as 'This island is abandoned to kitchen gardeners well skilled in the cultivation of salads', and 'Peasants emerge from the melon grounds to take the periwig and turn professor'.

But what Brown gave his appreciative clients was a purely English landscape. His predecessors had laid the foundations and the designed, natural landscape was fashionable. But until this point it had been primarily a foreign-inspired scene: a re-evaluation of nature based on a study of classical and renaissance art and a romanticized view of the Italian countryside. Brown was no painter, nor had he studied abroad. Indeed, when describing his design approach to the philanthropist Hannah More he used grammatical references: 'He told me he compared his art to literary composition. "Now there," said he, pointing his finger, "I make a comma, and there," pointing to another spot, "where a more decided turn is proper, I make a colon; at another part, where an interruption is desirable to break the view, a parenthesis; now a full stop, and then I begin another subject".'

Despite William Chambers' jealousy, the cost of Brown's work at Claremont – some £100,000 – was small beer compared with the cost of Lord Coventry's lifework at Croome Park in Worcestershire for which Brown also rebuilt the house, church and village. The final bill for that was about £400,000. But while Coventry spent his money over 61 years, Clive took only six (1768–74)!

Downhill Estate and Mussenden Temple, *CO. LONDONDERRY* *
FREDERICK AUGUSTUS HERVEY, 4TH EARL OF BRISTOL

Frederick Augustus Hervey, 4th Earl of Bristol and Bishop of both Cloyne and Derry (1730–1803), was a genial and occasionally mercurial chap with a passion for collecting. He obtained his bishoprics through the influence of his eldest brother, then Lord Lieutenant of Ireland, and was noted for religious tolerance, making him popular in Ireland. But, to be honest, his non-sectarian stance was rather more symptomatic of a none-too-strong devotion. He certainly enjoyed female company more than was appropriate for a man in his position and sometimes acted with a frivolity out of keeping with his station. On one infamous occasion he organized a curates' race along the sands at Downhill, awarding the winner a vacant benefice in his diocese!

Frivolous he may have been, but the Earl-Bishop was shrewd in financial matters and he certainly was extravagant in spending his lot. Keen to accrue funds to indulge his passions for architecture, travel and art, Frederick raised the income from his sees to £20,000 a year and supplemented that with rents from some 30,000 acres in England. Indeed he travelled so often and extravagantly that the many 'Hotel Bristols' across Europe were named after him. Many a journey was made to acquire more works for his already substantial art collection and his mania for collecting was such that when the French invaded Italy and occupied Rome in 1798, the Bishop's collection (which he had intended to ship home) was valued at £20,000.

In 1805, on a journey to Albano in Italy, he became ill and was carried to a small farm, where he subsequently died. The Catholic owners, realizing the patient was a heretic prelate, had banished him to an outhouse for fear his death in their home would bring bad luck. Frederick would no doubt have enjoyed the macabre final twist: his coffin was shipped back disguised as the packing case for an antique statue, in order to fool superstitious sailors who refused to have a corpse on board.

When it came to gardens, the Earl-Bishop was responsible for building Ickworth in Suffolk, as well as two gardens in Ireland – Ballyscullion in Co. Derry and, from c. 1775, Downhill. Perched high on the cliffs of Northern Ireland's most exposed piece of coastline, the Mussenden Temple is sadly the lone survivor of Frederick's creation at Downhill. Built in 1783–85 it is modelled on the circular Temple of Vesta at Tivoli, near Rome. Indeed, the original had so impressed him that he had actually purchased the ruins with the intention of shipping them back to Downhill, only to be thwarted at the last minute by the Italian authorities. The building takes its name from Frederick's cousin, the beautiful Mrs Frideswide Mussenden, with whom he was much taken. She died in 1785 at the age of 22 before the temple was completed and so it became her memorial rather than the place where she was to have entertained Frederick. Frederick established a room below the library in the Mussenden Temple for Catholic priests to say a weekly mass, once again showing his tolerance towards the Catholic Church.

The temple's aspect gives one indication of the challenges faced by Frederick in making his garden. One of his descendants noted in his autobiography that on one December day the wind was so strong that the servants could only get back from the temple to the house on hands and knees. Despite this rather unpromising situation, Frederick's letters are filled with the excitement of his gardening achievements. Writing in April 1783 to Arthur Young, his Suffolk neighbour, he extols the fresh air of Downhill and proudly boasts of his gardening triumphs:

'a tree is no longer a rarity, since above 200,000 have this winter been planted in the glens around my house. Come and enjoy the rapidity & the success with which I have converted sixty acres of moor by the medium of 200 spades into a green carpet sprinkled with white clover; am I not an adept in national dialect? Come and enjoy some mountains converted into arable, & grouse metamorphosed without a miracle into men. Come & teach a willing disciple and affectionate friend how to finish a work which he is barely able to begin ... And who do you think would consent to vegetate at Ickworth while he can direct such a laboratory at the Downhill?'

The fresh air and diversion of his garden clearly kept Frederick in fine fettle, for two years later – by which time 300,000 trees had been planted – he wrote to his daughter Mary, Countess of Erne, on 22 February 1785: 'I have had no gout this winter wch (sic) I attribute to Musick or harmony of mind. Everything is Redolent of Joy and youth & we commonly sit down to Table from 20 to 25. We have cold suppers, & a bottle of Champaign at each end of the table – the Songsters sing Ketches, & I go to bed which just now invites.'

Dunham Massey, *CHESHIRE* *
GEORGE BOOTH, 2ND EARL OF WARRINGTON

The majestic trees that fill the landscape here are rooted in excess as much as in good English soil. When George Booth, 2nd Earl of Warrington (1675–1758) added 100,000 oaks, elms and beeches to the park at Dunham Massey in Cheshire to form rides and avenues he was criticised for this extravagance, but according to *Hearts of Oak, the British Bulwarks* (1763), replied:

'Gentlemen, you may think it strange that I do these things; but I have the inward satisfaction in my own breast; the benefit of posterity; and my survivors will receive more than double the profit than by any other method I could possibly take for their interest.'

There was money to be had in land and timber, and landowners were not slow to bend the law to their own ends. From the 1760s onwards they voted into law the pernicious Enclosure Acts which empowered them to acquire more land by taking what had, until then, been common land. Thus farming yields, rents and incomes all increased for landowners, never mind that the small farmers were often forced off their land or denied their previous access to graze animals on the common.

> *There was money to be had in land and timber, and landowners were not slow to bend the law to their own ends*

Timber, as George Booth wasn't slow to realize, was another useful 'cash crop'. As John Torrington observed in his *Torrington Diaries* of 1789, the 'sowing of timber' had a dual role: it 'must not only afford infinite pleasure, but also an advancing adequate profit'. Until the late 17th century commercial forestry had been limited to the management of indigenous woodland, but thanks to pioneers such as William Windham I, who at Felbrigg Hall in Norfolk was one of the first landowners to establish plantations purely for profit in the 1670s, the 18th century became one of countrywide forestation.

Fenstanton, *HUNTINGDONSHIRE*
'CAPABILITY' BROWN

By 1762 'Capability' Brown had became sufficiently rich to turn down the £1,000 offered by the Duke of Leinster to come to Ireland, replying with tongue-in-cheek arrogance that 'he had not yet finished England'. He climbed the social ladder to the point of being appointed Royal Gardener to George III in 1764 and three years later bought into the minor gentry. In 1767, Lancelot, the humble gardener from Kirkhale purchased the small estate of Fenstanton for the sum of £13,000 and finally – and no doubt proudly – became a lord of the manor.

In 1767, Lancelot, the humble gardener from Kirkhale purchased the small estate of Fenstanton ... and finally – and no doubt proudly – became a lord of the manor

To what did 'Capability' Brown owe his phenomenal success? To his talent, but also to that lucky accident of being in the right place at the right time: in the mid-1700s, as Brown set up his drawing board, the British landscape was about to change dramatically and provide him with his canvas – and it was a very large one. Throughout the 18th century, Britain remained predominantly rural. The land remained the main wealth-producing powerhouse and provided its owners with social prestige and political power. Moreover, land ownership was pretty much a 'closed shop', changing hands only between landed families, and only through inter-marriage or inheritance. With skill, however, one could still 'buy into' at least landed gentry, if not aristocracy, by making a name – and a fortune – through a military career, trade, or banking. But it had to be a big fortune. According to garden historian Roger Turner in his book *Capability Brown and the Eighteenth-Century English Landscape* (1999), to run a country house, maintain landscape and to take part in all the activities associated with being a member of 'society' required an expenditure of about £10,000 per annum. This in turn required land holdings of 10–20,000 acres.

Gunby Hall, *LINCOLNSHIRE* *
PEREGRIN LANGTON MASSINGBERD

Massingberd was another landowner who took to tree-planting with a vengeance. In fact he kept a self-congratulatory tree-planting diary that shows he planted vast numbers of trees, some 420,000 between 1804 and 1827. In an entry from 1810 he pompously noted that the recently sown 16 acres of oak 'will be to my Grandson a noble & striking effect from the house & a means of procuring a very considerable additional share of comfort & luxury within the house'. It's perhaps satisfying to discover that 41 years later his grandson Algernon, the intended recipient of all this largesse, proceeded to go 'pussies road to ruin as hard as he could gallop'. Having rented out the house, he set off for a voyage up the Amazon, never to be seen again.

Milton Abbas, *DORSET*
JOSEPH DAMER, LORD MILTON, 1ST EARL OF DORCHESTER
'CAPABILITY' BROWN

Although Brown may have been admired and well-liked by his patrons, his habit of sweeping away inconvenient villages made him no friend to the common man, even if he was doing it 'under orders'. By far the most notorious relocation that Brown was involved in, though not directly responsible for, occurred at Milton Abbas. In 1780 Lord Milton (1718–98), owner of Milton Abbey, decided that the nearby village, Middleton, was getting in the way of the view. He commissioned Brown to design a new village, hidden away in a valley, with 36 nicely white-washed thatched cottages, each with its own patch of lawn and a chestnut tree (sadly the latter have long since gone). Some recalcitrant villagers did not want to move, and Milton 'encouraged' such ingratiates by the simple expedient of ordering the dam, which retained the water of his new lake, to be breached and thus flushing out the malcontents. The village of Middleton was subsequently demolished and, no doubt, the beautiful ornamental lake that Brown made was presumably a much more appealing prospect for Milton than looking at the 'riff-raff'.

Moor Park, *HEREFORDSHIRE*
ADMIRAL LORD ANSON, 'CAPABILITY' BROWN

George Anson (1697–1762) had commanded the fleet that defeated the French squadron commanded by Admiral de la Jonquière at the battle of Cape Finisterre, off north-west Spain, in 1747. He came back home with a promotion and significant prize money, using the latter to 'improve' Moor Park, from 1752 onwards. A sixteenth of the overall budget of £80,000 paid to make a sweeping landscape, complete with lake – some £5,000 – was paid to 'Capability' Brown to remove a small hill that was simply 'in the way'. One can't help wondering if Anson had got so accustomed to ordering ships from one place to another that he imagined hills could be moved in the same manner.

Petworth House, *SUSSEX* *
3RD LORD LECONFIELD, 'CAPABILITY' BROWN

'Capability' Brown's design for Petworth puts paid to the popular misconception that he never planted flowers. His 1752 recommendations for Charles Leconfield (1751–1837) included a 'gravel path through the mena(gerie) etc. with its borders adorned with Flowering Shrubs' and the 1753 bill from the nurseryman John Williamson lists 28 different plant types, including North American species.

For some privileged landowners, however, even a sumptuous 'Capability' Brown landscape was nothing to write home about, as John Wyndham, 4th Lord Egremont, wryly noted in his *Wyndham and Children First* (1969). When he took his bride-to-be to meet his uncle, the 3rd Lord Leconfield, she politely expressed admiration of the expansive 'Capability' Brown lake, and was rebuffed! His Lordship's blustering riposte was that her husband-to-be would be inheriting most of the lakes in the Lake District – some 35 square miles of water, and so what she was looking at was 'not a lake. It is a pond'.

> *'Capability' Brown's design for Petworth puts paid to the popular misconception that he never planted flowers*

Snowshill Manor, *GLOUCESTERSHIRE* *
CHARLES PAGET WADE

The 20th century saw many a 'strapped-for-cash' family of impeccable pedigree – and sometimes eccentric bent – hand their estate into the care of the National Trust. As Secretary of the Country Houses Committee from 1936 to 1951, James Lees-Milne criss-crossed the country with a missionary's zeal, cajoling the great-but-not-so-well-heeled into saving their 'stately piles' by donating them to the National Trust. His various diaries recount his encounters with keen observation and a raconteur's wit and he evidently had to contend with some very odd, unconventional and downright eccentric donors. So it was no mean feat to be accorded Lees-Milne's accolade 'the most eccentric National Trust donor I encountered', but Charles Paget Wade (1883–1956) was completely deserving of the title.

Wade first saw an advertisement for Snowshill while leafing through an old copy of *Country Life*, when serving in the trenches of the Western Front during World War I. After the war, Wade found the beautiful but derelict 16th-century manor was still on the market and purchased it in 1919. As well as rescuing the house, he began to collect obsessively. So keenly did he pursue this passion that the large house soon became full to over-flowing with his collections of every kind – bicycles, furniture, firemen's helmets, kitchen paraphernalia, Japanese lacquer cabinets, costumes (he enjoyed dressing up), suits of armour and more. To make more space for his objects, Wade was forced to move out into the adjacent Priest's House – although in the summer he sometimes slept in the lower garden house overlooking Well Court, which he shared with a stuffed heron. He was evidently quite a character and even Queen Mary pertly commented – on her visit to Snowshill in 1937 – that the most remarkable part of the collection was Mr Wade himself.

Perhaps Wade's eccentric obsessions could be put down to an unhappy childhood, mostly spent with his austere grandmother in Great Yarmouth in Norfolk. Here, there was 'seldom any laughter, and never any visitors or young folk'.

Here he also experienced his first garden 'a narrow dismal yard, pinched between dreary, drab walls' planted with a single *Euonymus*, a miserable *Saxifraga* x *urbium* (London Pride) and daffodils 'which all had their Latin names.' Given this gloomy start it is perhaps a wonder he went on to create such a beautiful garden at Snowshill. Made between 1920 and 1923, and with help from his architect friend M H Baillie Scott (1865–1945), the artfully designed and carefully arranged garden is a welcome antidote to the clutter inside the house. Situated on a steeply sloping Cotswold hillside is it s triumph of control and order that reflects Wade's ethos on garden-making. A garden, he believed, should be an extension of the house and, like the house, be made up of a series of 'outdoor rooms'. Each was to have its own character, to contrast with the others, but combine to create an harmonious whole. And in this 'The plan of a garden is much more important than the flowers in it.'

When, in 1920–23, Wade found time to make a garden, it was quite delightful – and a restful antidote to the clutter inside his house. The artfully arranged garden at Snowshill, designed with his friend Baillie Scott's willing assistance, is situated on a steeply sloping Cotswold hillside. A triumph of control and order, it reflects Wade's ethos on garden-making.

But the serious job of making a garden was not going to prevent the irrepressible Wade from having fun and playing with toys. Making a set of model houses (some of which survive) he created 'Wolf's Cove', a miniature Cornish fishing village set around the oval pool. This greatly impressed his friend John Betjeman who, in 1932, used it as a subject for an article in the *Architectural Review*. The piece bemoaned the loss of vanishing 'meirie England' and it was only in the last paragraph that Betjeman let on he was, after all, describing not a real village, but a half-inch scale model in Gloucestershire.

In 1946, to the great surprise of many and perhaps most of all to himself, the 63-year-old Wade married Mary McEwen Gore Graham, a lady 20 years his junior. Rather sweetly, a part of their courtship had consisted of kissing games in the garden at Snowshill. Ever the obsessive, Wade continued to add to his collection until 1951, when he presented the house and contents to the National Trust. Travelling from the West Indies, where he and his wife spent his later years, to be present at the ceremony he was described as 'still mischievous, waxy complexioned, a mediaeval face seen through the wood smoke'.

Wimpole Hall, *CAMBRIDGESHIRE* *
2ND EARL OF RADNOR, 2ND EARL OF OXFORD, 1ST EARL HARDWICKE; CHARLES BRIDGEMAN, 'CAPABILITY' BROWN

Greed can often manifest itself as a display of excess, wanting to have the biggest or the latest, most fashionable thing. A succession of owners took that approach with the house and gardens of Wimpole Hall, often proudly expending vast amounts of money on 'having it all'. Part of the problem was the 17th and 18th-century fashion for fiddly Franco-Dutch formal gardens. Although they weren't vast landscapes, they did cover numerous acres, and were packed with costly flowers and features. In the words of Stephen Switzer (1682–1745) they were 'a Burthen too great for the biggest Estate and not at all answerable to the needless Expence that is laid out upon them'. Indeed the avaricious desire to have such gardens occasionally caused the

Walpole (on 'Capability' Brown): 'so closely did he copy nature that his works will be mistaken'

ruination of men. In 1710, the rake and gold-digger Charles Robartes (1660–1723), 2nd Earl of Radnor was forced to sell Wimpole Hall. Inheriting a £20,000 fortune (and the property itself) in the wake of his wife's premature death, he'd blown most of the money on the house and formal garden. But he did build a very nice orangery.

Robartes's successor at Wimpole was Edward Harley, 2nd Earl of Oxford (1689–1741) , who married Henrietta Cavendish-Holles in the ornate ante-room on 31 August 1713. A staunch Tory, and son of Tory chief minister Robert Harley, 1st Earl of Oxford, who found his political position usurped during his absence from London when, following Queen Anne's death in 1714 and the Hanoverian succession, the opposing Whigs brought down the Tory oligarchy and advocated reform. Excluded from office because of his political beliefs, Edward dedicated his prodigious energies to developing Wimpole instead. As well as being a passionate collector of books and art, he engaged the noted landscape designer Charles Bridgeman (d.1738) to extend the gardens. Things didn't always go to plan: in October 1721, during the construction of a new bason (a terraced amphitheatre in the grounds) a newspaper reported that 'the workmen as they were digging up the ground for this latter, dug up the Bones of fourteen human corpses most of them having large Nails drove through their Skulls'. Sadly Edward fell victim to the same problem as his predecessor: in 1739, after a quarter of a century of excessive spending and, eventually taking refuge in drink, he faced the galling necessity to sell Wimpole to Whig Lord Chancellor, 1st Earl Hardwicke (1690–1764).

A generation later, Philip, the 2nd Earl (1720–90) and his wife, Jemima, Marchioness of Grey employed 'Capability' Brown at Wimpole, having previously used his services at Wrest Park in Bedfordshire. We know that Brown was paid £3,380, but his original plans have long since been lost. Helpfully, a depiction of how he intended the landscape to appear was recorded on six dessert plates, part of a spectacular Wedgwood dinner service commissioned by Catherine the Great,

Empress of Russia in 1774. Now in the Hermitage Museum, St Petersburg, they proved an invaluable aid to restoration work. At the outset of Brown's assignment Lady Grey wrote to her daughter in September 1769:

> '"Break off, Break off, we tread enchanted Ground" – is almost literally true with me at present. Mr. Brown has been leading me such a Fairy Circle & his Magic Wand has raised such landscapes to the Eye – not visionary for they were all there but his touch has brought them out with the same effect as a Painter's Pencil upon Canvass – that after having hobbled over rough Ground to Points that I had never seen before, for two Hours, I return half Tired, & Foot sore.'

Brown became so phenomenally successful quickly because times were changing fast and he moved with them. As he set up his drawing board, the British landscape was about to change dramatically and provide him with his canvas. His vision of a romantic and romanticized England was implicitly understood by his contemporaries and we still subliminally respond positively to it today when we gaze over the 'natural' countryside of downland Britain, unaware that most of it has been 'improved' by Brown and his adherents. Indeed his landscapes have been called England's greatest contribution to world art. Horace Walpole's (1717–97) eulogy on hearing of Brown's death in 1783 perfectly encapsulates the genius of the man, his work, and the age: 'Such was the effect of his genius that when he was the happiest man he will be least remembered, so closely did he copy nature that his works will be mistaken.'

Landowners were anxious to maximize their profits and the Brownian landscape also saved money

But, to bring the landscape back down to earth, a desire to turn a profit came into it as well. Landowners were anxious to maximize their profits and the Brownian landscape also saved money. It was far less expensive to maintain than all the topiary clipping, fruit tree training, seasonal planting, bulb cultivation, gravel raking, waterworks maintenance and parterre tweaking necessitated by the formal gardens of the 17th century.

Nevertheless, at Wimpole Hall old habits died hard. Just for the record, the decadent 5th Earl (1836–1897), who was none-too-respectfully known as 'the Glossy Peer' and 'Champagne Charlie' – and had, according to Lady Battersea, a 'pleased-with-himself-and-the-world-expression' – was forced to relinquish Wimpole in 1894 having run up debts (mostly through gambling) to the staggering tune of £300,000 in his 15 years of ownership. Following over 40 years of decline and decay it was Rudyard Kipling's daughter, Elsie Bambridge (1896–1976) and her husband George, who in 1936 saved Wimpole and later gave it to the National Trust. Kipling cautioned his daughter on his only visit 'Bird, I hope you have not bitten off more than you can chew!' Ironically, it was Rudyard's posthumous royalties that paid most of the restoration bills. Nonetheless, Elsie was possessive of her purchase. On one occasion when discovering picnickers in her park, she ordered the chauffeur to pack a hamper, follow the trespassers home, and retaliate by taking tea on their lawn!

generosity

*'**Kindness** towards others.'*

Until the 20th century, it was a given that 'a gentleman
did not work', and, using their wealth to live lavishly, life
was good for the landed. Within this sector of society
generosity was manifest in the endless exchange of
hospitality (and garden plants!), which, of course, also
offered ample scope for displays of pride. However, there
were those who also displayed a social conscience and
made displays of generosity to those less fortunate.
Taking care of one's staff and allowing the 'riff-raff'
into one's garden were two popular forms of showing
generosity. Occasionally, though, the 'riff-raff' proved
to be jolly ungrateful.

Arlington Court, DEVON *
ROSALIE CHICHESTER

Eccentric traveller, Rosalie Chichester (1865–1949), took an original
approach to generosity. Inspired by her visits to National Parks in
Australia and New Zealand, she decided to combine conservation and
philanthropy. In the 1930s she converted her father's 1860s shooting
landscape into the Reserve, a wildlife park in which all hunting was
banned. Rosalie's love of animals created an eclectic menagerie of
canaries, budgerigars, parrots and peacocks, Shetland ponies, Jacob's
sheep and dogs. Here she held lessons for local schoolchildren and she
also opened up the grounds to the general public. At one time a visit
to Arlington was so popular that in excess of 300 visitors a day would
travel up by charabanc from Ilfracombe for a nice 'day out'.

Ascott, *BUCKINGHAMSHIRE* *
BARON LEOPOLD DE ROTHSCHILD

A somewhat sycophantic article from the *Gardeners' Chronicle* in 1896 catalogues Leopold de Rothschild's (1845–1917) munificence at Ascott where, like many socially-minded landowners of the time, he provided both recreational and educational facilities for his staff:

> 'For the recreation of those employed on the estate, as well as for others, a well-prepared cricket-ground has been laid down. During the winter evenings, classes are held for carving in wood, etc., thus affording occupation for all who in any way desire or seek self-improvement. The bothy (accommodation for junior garden staff) is a model of what such erections should be, being well appointed inside, and having a picturesque exterior also.'

Batemans, *EAST SUSSEX* *
RUDYARD KIPLING

As host to the Burwash local village flower show, Rudyard Kipling (1865–1936) generously opened his garden gates to the house and garden he loved so much. However, he did wryly remark that:

> 'This means that the entire population will decant itself into and over our garden and the next field; will dance on the lawn till 9.30 p.m. and will generally possess and devastate the whole place with the cheeriest good will in the world'. The day after the show he continued, with good humour and grace: 'Oh we had our flower show yesterday in the one day of decent weather since June. Over 1000 folk turned up and we were at it from 7 a.m. till 9.30 p.m. And today the lawns look as tho' they had been rented out to all the bulls of Bashan. But no damage and much mirth. I wish you could have seen it. It was so curiously local and self-contained … At the end we all congratulated each other on the way "our" show had gone off.'

Kipling: 'Oh we had our flower show yesterday ... today the lawns look as tho' they had been rented out to all the bulls of Bashan'

Rudyard, or 'Rud', and his wife, Caroline loved Bateman's and enjoyed sharing it with their guests. They had fallen in love with it on first sight, in 1902, when Rudyard – one of the country's earliest motorists – had driven them, in their steam-powered car, 'down an enlarged rabbit-hole of a lane'. On entering Batemans 'We ... felt her Spirit and Feng Shui to be good'. Kipling duly purchased the property for a mere £9,300, the seller later wryly observing that if he, like Kipling, had foreseen how the car would come to dominate travel, he would certainly have doubled the asking price.

Whereas Kipling has been roundly censured for imperialistic beliefs, his qualities as a writer, quite apart from his subject matter, have come to receive their proper due. After all, Kipling was a best selling author in his time, and in 1907 became the first Englishman to receive the Nobel Prize for Literature. He spent some of his £7,700 prize money on making his garden, which inspired one of his most famous poems 'The Glory of the Garden'. The garden also appeared in other works: the mulberry garden was the setting for the opening scene of 'A Doctor of Medicine', a children's story published in *Rewards and Fairies* (1910); the mill, the site of a real life murder and tragic death, appeared in *Puck of Pook's Hill* and in the story 'Below the Mill Dam'. Kipling evidently enjoyed a bit of garden therapy too: he wrote to a friend: 'the wife and I had a glorious day in the garden alone ... building a

Right: Celebrated writer Rudyard Kipling in an etching by William Strang.

little dry stone wall … We knocked off, stiff, sore (stones aren't easy to handle), pretty dirty, but quite happy. Why is it that one gets more joy over a job like that than "literature"?'

> **Kipling: 'the wife and I had a glorious day in the garden alone … building a little dry stone wall … pretty dirty, but quite happy. Why is it that one gets more joy over a job like that than "literature"?'**

Generous hosts the Kiplings may have been, but when it came to politely getting rid of visitors who had outstayed their welcome, Kipling had a novel approach. The sundial at Bateman's is inscribed 'It is later than you think': it was to this ornament that, according Kipling's wife Carrie, 'Rud always brings his guests to read (the inscription) when he thinks they should be going home.'

Blickling Hall, *NORFOLK* *
LADY LOTHIAN

Lady Lothian of Blickling Hall was another employer with a social conscience. *The Garden* wrote in 1903 that she 'had such a tender heart for the gardeners who had grown old in her service that, instead of pensioning them off, she kept them about the place to do light work'. Until her death, a staff of fifteen ex-gardeners was retained at Blickling. So perhaps the garden was rather crowded at times!

Claremont Landscape Garden, *SURREY* *
THOMAS PELHAM-HOLLES, 1ST DUKE OF NEWCASTLE-UNDER-LYNE

Thomas Pelham-Holles, 1st Duke of Newcastle (1693–1768), was a generous host, with a legendary reputation both for his hospitality and the company he kept. Although writing later in the century, Walpole's description of the garden at Claremont, dressed for a fête in 1763, offers another intimation of how exotic, exciting and romantic grand scale parties, such as those hosted by Thomas, must have been:

'From thence (the Belvedere) we passed in to the wood, and the ladies formed a circle of chairs before the mouth of a cave, which was overhung to a vast height with wood bines, lilacs and laburnums, and dignified with tall stately cypresses. On the descent of the hill were placed French horns; the abigails, servants and neighbours wandering below by the river; in short, it was Parnassus, as Watteau would have painted it.'

Regular guests to Claremont included Kings George I and II, other members of the Royal family and nobility, and all manner of politicians and ambassadors. All were treated to a garden tour, a sophisticated dining experience in a garden house, or perhaps the entertainment of a cock-fight held in the grass amphitheatre,

the Comte d'Artois contrived to import a wild boar which he planned to hunt … which was finally cornered and killed in Esher High Street

designed by Bridgeman. Occasionally, though, the unfortunate consequences of Thomas' hospitality became the stuff of legend, too, and were one especially boozy night of 1742 repeated today, the tabloids would have a field day. On this occasion, their Lords Bath, Carteret, and Limerick, together with all their servants, got so blindingly drunk that on the way home they overturned their coach crossing Richmond Park and the whole party had to be rescued by the Earl of Orford's coachman.

Just over a century later, in 1848, Claremont was the point of departure for another ill-fated expedition. By this juncture, Queen Victoria had generously granted the estate as a refuge to the exiled French Royals. Bored with a life of exile, and in an attempt to enliven his dull existence a bit, the Comte d'Artois contrived to import a wild boar which he planned to hunt. Sadly, he was not as cunning as his quarry, which was finally cornered and killed in Esher High Street by some more competent locals.

Cragside House, *NORTHUMBERLAND* *
PRINCE AND PRINCESS OF WALES, LORD ARMSTRONG

In August 1884, at a time when Buckingham Palace still didn't have electricity, William George, 1st Lord Armstrong, generously greeted his visitors, the Prince and Princess of Wales – later Edward VII (1810–1900) and Queen Alexandra (1841–1910) – with 'Ten thousand small glass lamps … hung amongst the rocky hillside … and an almost equal number of Chinese lanterns … swung across leafy glades, and continued pendant from tree to tree in sinuous lines, miles in extent', and topped off the event with a huge firework display.

But sometimes, however generous you are, people just don't show any gratitude. In the 1890s Lord Armstrong made the park available for use by 'trippers', but was subsequently forced to erect a sign, rather angrily stating 'Notice – The vulgar practice of cutting or scratching names or letters upon the stones or seats is strictly forbidden, no smoking allowed'.

Erddig, *NORTHUMBERLAND* *
THE YORKE FAMILY

The somewhat unconventional Yorke family were generous in their respect for their staff and treated them as fondly-regarded members of the family – often hanging their portraits on the wall. Head Gardener Thomas Pritchard and his successor, James Phillips were captured for posterity, in paint and on film respectively. The latter also received the honour of being immortalised in doggerel verse:

'Our Gardener here, James Phillips see,
A Bachelor of Husbandry,
Who did from garden-boy become
The finished grower of the Plum
Scarce ever absent from our ground
Then only some few miles around.
This Garden formed his chief delight,
And was as Eden in his sight.
Old-fashioned, in his notions, he
With foreign names, did not agree
'Quatre-Saisons' 'Quarter-Sessions' meant,
The 'Bijou' as the 'By Joe' went,
'Glory to die John' was the Rose,
Which each as 'Gloire de Dijon' knows.
No Green-house here 'twas his advice
The Antique Frames would well suffice.'

Knole, *KENT* *
MORTIMER SACKVILLE-WEST, 1ST BARON SACKVILLE

At Knole, the Sackville family had allowed their private medieval deer park (a rare survivor of its type) to become a short cut used by nearby villagers; residents of Sevenoaks came to believe access was their right. With numbers swollen by day-trippers taking the train from London, it all became too much for Mortimer, 1st Baron Sackville (1820–1888) who, in 1883 blocked the main gate to all but pedestrians. Such was the local indignation and resentment that on the night of the 18th June 1884 a mob tore down the barriers, and singing 'Rule Britannia', dumped them in a pile on Mortimer's doorstep. The following evening more abuse was hurled, a few windows smashed, and the Fawke Gate forced allowing the mob to tauntingly ride back and forth through the now open entrance. Lord Sackville was not amused!

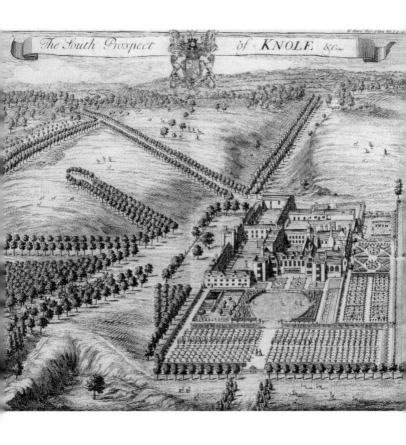

Above: A bird's eye view of Knole, engraved by
Johannes Kip c.1705. The Sackville family allowed
the grounds to be used as a short cut by local villagers.

Knightshayes Court, *DEVON* *
SIR JOHN HEATHCOAT AMORY

Shows of generosity and kindness to tenants and workers were important duties of care for landowners and gentry. In 1872 Sir John Heathcoat Amory (1829–1914) held a dinner at Knightshayes Court for the employees from his lace factory in nearby Tiverton. The company had been founded by his grandfather, John Heathcoat, who had patented a machine that revolutionised lace-making. Following a Luddite attack on his premises in Loughborough in 1816, John relocated his lace factory to Tiverton, where he built it up to be the world's largest. Many of his faithful workers had walked the 321km (200 miles) from Loughborough to Tiverton to work for him and both John and his grandson always cherished their loyalty. The party concerned was a large affair: the 1,300 workers processed from the factory, through streets decorated with flags and bunting, to arrive at Knightshayes – where three marquees filled with food awaited the grateful throng. According to a report in the local paper, after the dinner a foreman proposed the health of Mr Amory and photographers were kept busy taking group photographs. Then 'At 8 o'clock one of the two bands engaged played "God Save the Queen" before they all marched off back to town'.

Mount Stewart House, *CO. DOWN* *
7TH MARQUESS AND MARCHIONESS OF LONDONDERRY

In 1921 Charles, 7th Marquess of Londonderry (1878–1949) and his wife, Edith (1878–1959), moved to Mount Stewart in Northern Ireland. The Marchioness's first impressions were hardly encouraging: 'I thought the house and surroundings were the dampest, darkest and saddest places I had ever stayed in.' But Edith quickly realised that the sheltered site and mild climate was perfect for growing plants and she developed a garden as renowned for its collection of unusual inhabitants as its diversity of compartments and styles.

Prior to the move the couple had lived in London where the beautiful Edith, as warm and cultured as she was outgoing and generous, was a celebrated hostess. During World War I she had founded the Ark Club, a regular gathering of friends who met at Londonderry House to dine, exchange views and relax. Now, as a memorial to the Ark Club over which she had presided in her guise as Circe the Sorceress, Edith created the Dodo Terrace at Mount Stewart. Here, cast in their cement glory stand the zoomorphic alter egos of certain members, including Charley the Cheetah (her husband), Freddy the Frog (Frederick, Lord Dufferin), and Linky the Lemur (Lord Hugh Cecil).

But the garden was also home to live real animals, partly due to some generous – and not entirely successful – gift giving. The flamingos that graced the lake were a present from King Faud of Egypt and when one escaped it was bagged by a local duck shooter. The Stanley cranes, however, were swiftly removed, due to their tendency to indiscriminately attack all and sundry. Fortunately, the younger daughter of the house, Lady Mairi, was allowed to keep the marmoset and ring-tailed lemur purchased at Harrods.

Edith had more success with topiary. Her account has it that the figures in the Shamrock Garden are 'a complete caricature of an ancient hunting scene supposed to represent the family of Stuart ... The figures, with the exception of the oracle, which was copied from an ancient tombstone, were taken from Mary I of England's Book of Hours'. But Lady Mairi maintained that the figures in the boat were supposed to represent her parents, their three younger daughters and the boatman Edmund Brock, the latter clutching a bottle of whiskey!

Edith benefited from the generosity of many of the great gardeners of the day, in making her garden. She corresponded with, among others, Norah Lindsay (see Hidcote Manor, page 102), Sir Herbert Maxwell, who made his garden at Monreith in Wigtownshire (one of the three Counties which make up Dumfries-Galloway), and Sir John Ross, who gardened at Rostrevor House in Co. Down and, in 1920, had the largest private collection of plants in Ireland. They sent her seeds and plants to help to build her garden at Mount Stewart, where the different compartments – the parterres, the Spanish Garden, the Mairi Garden, the Dodo Terrace, the Shamrock Garden and Tir Nan Og – were all filled with a rich mix of plants and the lily wood featured rare plants from all over the world, in particular Australasia, South America, Indo-China and the Himalayas. An early believer in organic gardening techniques, Edith was influenced in her thinking by the garden writer, Eleanour Sinclair Rhode, who also sent her seeds. In

1920 Edith sought advice from Gertrude Jekyll, the most influential gardener of her age and probably of the 20th century. Jekyll designed the Sunken Garden and offered planting suggestions, but it has to be said that not all were followed.

As well as receiving plants, Edith was always a generous donor in turn, and her gardening diaries are filled with long and frequent lists of 'plants to be given away'. Recipients of her generosity included Queen Alexandra and Queen Elizabeth, the late Queen Mother. But as a lover of rhododendrons, she was also a fiercely competitive exhibitor at Royal Horticultural Society shows, regularly winning prizes for her blooms, which were carefully packed and, accompanied by a gardener, dispatched by sea or air to London.

Edith was also one of the first owners to generously open her garden to the public for charity. In 1926 the entertainments available for the visitors to enjoy included classical dances in the Sunken Garden, Irish dancing in the Italian Garden (with music played by the house piper, no less), booths on the north lawn selling sweets, Japanese parasols and the work of ex-servicemen, Edmund Brock – who was apparently skilled at 'transposing signatures into faces'. Four palmists were scattered at various points in the gardens, there was bridge in the house and music played in the Hall. And all this came cheap – entrance was a mere 2s 6d.

pride

'A feeling of **deep pleasure** or
      satisfaction derived from achievements,
            qualities, or possessions. Having an
excessively high opinion of yourself.'

Certain owners created grand gardens to become the
subject of admiration and simultaneously be 'in with
the in set', and, so very proud of themselves and their
position, they were just as odious as their modern day
counterparts. Thankfully, albeit occasionally, the age-old
adage 'pride comes before a fall' came into play with very
satisfying results – although this raises the question
whether *schadenfreude* ought to be a deadly sin! However,
many garden makers were less calculating and made their
gardens for the simple reason that they liked gardening,
were proud to demonstrate their talents and enjoyed the
attention and plaudits that it generated and received.

Bodiam Castle, *EAST SUSSEX* *
SIR EDWARD DALYNGRIGGE

Bodiam, or 'Bodyham' as it was originally known, was erected in the
late 14th century by Sir Edward Dalyngrigge (d.1390), a member of an
old-established Sussex family who had married money and gained
further rank through services to Court and Parliament. Not content
with that, he substantially increased his wealth by participating in the
Hundred Years War against France, as a member of a 'free company' – a
private army of mercenaries, under the nominal command of the king
– led by Sir Robert Knolly, a ruthless man with a notorious reputation.

Returning home in 1377, proud Sir Edward wanted to show off his new standing and wealth with the status symbol of the day – a 'castle of chivalry' – and he pulled a bit of a fast one in order to get his way. Playing on the fears of a retaliatory invasion by the French he applied for, and was granted in October 1385, a royal licence to 'crenellate'. But rather than fortify his existing manor house, as was expected, he picked a new site of rather questionable defensive merit. Then he artfully placed his 'des res' castle in the centre of a carefully designed system of moat and artificial ponds so that, to the approaching visitor, the effect was an Arthurian spectacle of a fantasy castle rising ethereally and Excalibur-like from a reflecting watery expanse.

Vita Sackville-West (1892–1962) had a very soft spot for what she called her 'beloved Bodiam', but had to swallow her pride and settle for Sissinghurst as second best. When Bodiam came on the market in 1925 for £30,000 she just couldn't afford it.

Chastleton House, *OXFORDSHIRE* *
WALTER JONES, JOHN & DOROTHY WHITMORE-JONES

In 1602 Walter Jones (d.1632) paid Robert Catesby £4,000 for Chastleton, money that Catesby was not too proud to take, since he had been fined more than half that sum for his involvement in the Earl of Essex's 1601 rebellion against Elizabeth I. Sadly Catesby remained impoverished, and rebellious too: four years later he became the leader of the Gunpowder Plot, and died during the raid on Holbeache House in Staffordshire on 8 November 1605.

But Walter Jones was certainly proud enough to want to climb the social ladder. A wealthy professional who had 'bettered himself' by setting up as a country gent, he used family money from the wool trade to train as a successful lawyer. Not content with that, he'd simultaneously developed a political career as town clerk, and subsequently MP, for Worcester. The house and ornamental Best Garden at Chastleton House were created by Jones from about 1607.

The Best Garden was designed as a *hortus conclusus* or 'secret garden', to be looked down on from the Great Chamber and entered only from the Great Parlour. This made it the private realm of the master of the house and his invited guests, wholly separate from the other garden compartments, which included an orchard, a vegetable garden, and the subsequently famous bowling green (see Chastleton, page 113). Modifications in later centuries have somewhat destroyed this sense of the garden's enclosure, and the topiary that is such a striking feature today was probably replanted in 1883. The now amorphous blobs of shrubbery originally included a cake stand, a horse, a lyrebird, a cat, a ship in full sail, a tea pot, a peacock and a crown. Even so, the essence of the Best Garden remains and it is a rare example of its type.

Another planting oddity at Chastleton is found in the wider parkland, where later owners took to the 'political planting' of trees. Arthur Jones I planted the Restoration Oaks in celebration of the return of the monarchy in 1660, while his Jacobite great-grandson Henry planted patriotic stands of Scots Pine in the 18th century and in the 19th century John and Dorothy Whitmore-Jones sowed acorns from the famous Boscobel Royal Oak.

Cliveden, *BUCKINGHAMSHIRE* *
FREDERICK, PRINCE OF WALES

Cliveden was leased by Frederick, Prince of Wales (1707–51) between 1739 and 1751, and he regularly staged plays, concerts and pantomimes in Bridgeman's magnificent grass amphitheatre. On one such occasion, on 1 August 1740, the premier of the *Masque of Alfred* was performed: written specifically for the Prince by Thomas Arne, it contains the famous aria 'Rule Britannia'. So flattered was Frederick at the end of the first performance that he immediately ordered an encore. But, as a newspaper reported 'the rain falling very heavy, oblig'd them to break off before it was half over'. As they say, pride often comes before a fall, and in this case the British weather behaved with opprobrium.

Ham House, *SURREY* *
ELIZABETH DYSART & JOHN MAITLAND, DUKE OF LAUDERDALE

In 1678 John Evelyn wrote in his journal: 'After dinner I walked to Ham to see the house and garden of the Duke of Lauderdale, which is indeed inferior to few of the best villas in Italy itself, the house furnished like a great Prince's, the parterres, flower garden, orangeries, groves, avenues, courts, statues, perspectives, fountains, aviaries and all this at the banks of the sweetest river in the world, must needs be surprising'.

The 17th-century formal garden at Ham House had been lost, but has been restored to its former glory by the National Trust. An impressive and opulent creation, it was originally the brainchild of two very self-satisfied characters: Elizabeth Dysart (1628–1698) and her second husband, John Maitland, Duke of Lauderdale (1616–1682). Elizabeth, like many powerful women through the ages, has enjoyed a mixed press. Described by one contemporary as 'restless in her ambition, profuse in her expense and of a most ravenous covetousness', another observer, Bishop Burnet wrote: 'she was a woman of great beauty, but of far greater parts. She had a wonderful quickness of apprehension and an amazing vivacity in conversation … She was violent in everything she set about, a violent friend, but a still more violent enemy'. Either way, she had a colourful life and she certainly liked to spend money.

Following the execution of Charles I in 1649, Elizabeth played her cards almost too well: Protector Cromwell became so fond of her that gossip spread and he was obliged to break off their friendship. But at the same time she was an active member of the secret society known as the 'Sealed Knot' which worked covertly for Charles II's restoration. This event, when it came, brought not only rewards and favours, but also the return from exile of her married lover, John Maitland. In 1665 Elizabeth inherited Ham House from her father, in 1669 her husband died, followed in 1671 by John Maitland's wife. Within six weeks of the latter, John – who was in 1672 created Duke of Lauderdale – and Elizabeth had married. Bishop Burnet paints an unattractive portrait of Lauderdale, as an ugly man with a rough manner whose 'temper was intolerable, for he was haughty beyond all expression to all who had expectances from him, but abject where himself had any; and so violently passionate that he often times, upon slight occasions, ran himself into fits like madness'. Yet Charles II, who loved beauty, seems not to have been put off and Lauderdale became the 'L' in the 'Cabal' ministry– the five-man group behind which Charles II governed in the late 1660s and early 1670s.

Equipped with the fortune made by the avaricious Lauderdale, Elizabeth refurbished both the house and the gardens in the most fashionable and grand style. The terrace to the south of the house boasted painted wooden benches and stools, and pots in stone and gilded lead. From there one descended to eight square grass plats (lawns), each ornamented with a centrally positioned sculpture. Both terrace and lawns were probably embellished in the summer months by some 300 pots containing tender (and expensive) trees: oleander, myrtles, oranges, lemons, and pomegranates. Beyond that was the formal wilderness – a rectangular area divided into 16 geometrically shaped compartments by straight paths bordered by hedges and trees – while to the west was a large kitchen garden divided into 32 compartments and an orangery (in which the tender trees would have been over-wintered). To the east was the Cherry Garden, home to the most expensive and intricate devices, including knots, a banqueting house, twin viewing platforms and the Melancholy Walk. Ill-health forced Lauderdale out of office in 1680 and once he had lost power he also lost his pensions. Elizabeth was forced to curb her expenditure, but debts already run up meant she was forced to pawn her jewels and paintings. After John's death she died at Ham House in very humble circumstances, penniless and 'disfurnished'. Nevertheless, her ghost is reputed still to walk the corridors of the house and doubtlessly interacts with some of the other resident ghosts of both house and garden; Ham House is one of the 'most haunted' properties owned by the National Trust.

Prior Park, *BATH, SOMERSET* *
RALPH ALLEN, 'CAPABILITY' BROWN, ALEXANDER POPE

Not all landscapes of pride were professionally designed, although it helps to have knowledgeable friends: both the poet Alexander Pope (1688–1744) and, later, the landscape designer 'Capability' Brown advised Allen (1694–1763) on the design of his garden, Pope having made his own mini-landscape of five acres at Twickenham in 1719.

After making his first fortune re-organizing the postal system, Cornish entrepreneur Ralph Allen made his second from Bath stone – in the process developing the water navigation system that enabled him to transport it to London. Allen was also a philanthropist, endowing charities and helping to found the Mineral Water Hospital in his adopted city of Bath. A 'wannabe' country gent, Allen began to make his intimate landscape garden at Prior Park in 1734, with help from Alexander Pope. As he looked out from his grand mansion at the sweeping view over 28 steeply sloping acres, Allen must have felt very proud indeed. Not only was he looking down on the great, the good, and the titled, but the beautiful city below had been built with 'his' stone.

Sissinghurst Castle Garden, *KENT* *
VITA SACKVILLE-WEST, HAROLD NICOLSON

Pride can be a powerful motivating force for people who are eager to prove themselves. Vita Sackville-West was descended from a long line of eccentrics and she was a Sackville to the core: her grandfathers were brothers and her parents were cousins. Her mother Victoria, one of five illegitimate children of Lionel Sackville by the Spanish dancer Pepita, behaved extraordinarily to her daughter. One minute she would spoil Vita with huge jewels, and the next would cruelly demand them back, accusing her of theft. She was the same when it came to money, holding ostentatious house parties one moment, the next moment writing to Vita on loo paper stolen from the 'Ladies' in Harrods.

Vita loved the family home of Knole in Kent with an 'atavistic passion' but, although she was the eldest

The house and garden at Sissinghurst became the outlet for Vita's creativity, pride and passion – and perhaps a way of diverting her fiery, sometimes jealous nature

child when her father died in 1928, the law of primogeniture meant that the house passed to the eldest son – so she missed out due to a 'technical fault', as she put it. Instead, she and husband Harold Nicolson (1886–1968) bought the shambling 16th-century ruin of Sissinghurst Castle in Kent for £12,375 in 1930. The house and garden at Sissinghurst became the outlet for Vita's creativity, pride and passion

– and perhaps a way of diverting her fiery, sometimes jealous nature. As her husband commented perceptively, Sissinghurst was 'a succession of privacies: the forecourt, the first arch, the main court, the tower arch, the lawn, the orchard. All a series of escapes from the world, giving the impression of cumulative escape.' Yet, like its famous White Garden, its effect as much due to the subtle green of the foliage display as the great show of white blooms, so the garden at Sissinghurst was also the product of a deep symbiosis, in this case between husband and wife. Harold's classically-inspired and generally underappreciated formal structure providing the supporting stage set for Vita's flamboyant and romantic shows of plants. Indeed it was no different in their private lives: while both were bisexual, they enjoyed a happy, if somewhat unconventional, marriage of 49 years. But while Harold's homosexual affairs were clandestine, Vita's were far more public.

Stourhead, *WILTSHIRE* *
HENRY HOARE II

> 'And Happy he, who in a Country Seat,
> From Storms of Bus'ness finds a Retreat …
> Where all around delightful Landskips lie,
> And pleasing Prospects entertain his Eye.'

René Rapin penned these joyful words in his *Of Gardens* (trans. James Gardiner, 1706), and they have a prophetic ring when applied to the garden-making of Henry Hoare II. In the same time frame that 'Capability' Brown forged his career as a professional landscaper, this proud amateur created the sublime and symbolic classical landscape at Stourhead. With lofty conifers and colourful rhododendrons as 19th-century additions, the garden today is different from the concept conceived by Hoare (1705–85), who inherited wealth from his banker father in 1724. Known within the family as 'the Magnificent', young Henry II was both sensible banker and wealthy, fashionable socialite. In the company of similarly privileged young men he drank, hunted, and made merry until he finally came to the conclusion that his 'gay and dissolute style of life' was having an adverse effect on his health. Banking on the other hand, especially lending money to many of the landowners who were improving their estates (as well as to landscape designers like William Kent), brought nothing but profit and enabled Henry to develop his own estate at Stourhead, which he inherited in 1738 on the death of his mother, necessitating his return from a Grand Tour of Europe.

In 1743 his second wife died (his first having died in childbirth), leaving him with three children (sadly, they subsequently all pre-deceased him). Perhaps as a diversion from his immediate grief, Hoare determinedly set about making an Arcadian idyll inspired by the landscapes, architecture, literature and art that had so enthralled him on his visit to Italy. Although allegorically representing Aeneas's wanderings before founding Rome, any attempts at authenticity were abandoned in favour of a juxtaposition of classical temples, tempered natural landscape, a Chinese alcove, Turkish tent, hermitage, the Bristol High Cross (transported from the city and re-erected on his estate) and the picturesque village of Stourton. Moreover, Hoare mixed up classical, pagan and staunch Protestant imagery in Alfred's Tower, which he erected on the ridge above the garden to commemorate Alfred the Great supposedly raising his standard at Stourton en route to the Battle of Edington in 878. Completed in 1772, the tower also makes a deliberately political point: Hoare celebrates both the 'Great King' who put his country first and the accession of George III in 1760. This George, Hoare hoped, would behave more like Alfred than his Hanoverian ancestors who had used England to secure their own self-interests on the Continent.

Stowe Landscape Gardens, *BUCKINGHAMSHIRE* *
LORD COBHAM, CHARLES BRIDGEMAN, WILLIAM KENT,
'CAPABILITY' BROWN

In so many cases the making of a grand landscape or garden came from an ostentatious desire to cry out 'look at me and at my garden, and at the message within!' One of the biggest of all 18th-century landscapes, Stowe, almost deafens the visitor, so grand is the creation of its proud owner, Lord Cobham (1665–1749). Cobham, the 4th Baronet Temple, inherited Stowe in 1697. Later renowned as an MP, Cobham first became celebrated as a soldier serving under the Duke of Marlborough in the wars against the French. Appointed Colonel in 1701 when aged only 26, he rose to be Lieutenant-General by 1710 and was called 'the greatest Whig in the army' by Jonathan Swift. After a temporary fall from grace

In so many cases the making of a grand landscape or garden came from an ostentatious desire to cry out 'look at me and at my garden, and at the message within!'

in 1713 when he was dismissed from the army by the Tories, he was favoured once again in 1714 by the new King, George I, who raised him to Baron Cobham and made him a Viscount four years later. His fortune, derived from his military income, a number of sinecures and successful ventures and a £20,000 dowry brought by his wife Anne Halsey (a brewing heiress whom he wed in 1715), funded his gardening ambitions.

Cobham began his garden in earnest in 1714, with the arrival at Stowe of the 18th century's first and perhaps least remembered landscape designer, Charles Bridgeman. Before arriving at Stowe, Bridgeman had worked as an assistant supervisor on the gardens then under construction at Blenheim, where the magnificent palace was being erected by Sir John Vanbrugh (1664–1726), who later also built Stowe House. Stowe is one of Bridgeman's earliest commissions and arguably his finest. Such was the family's ambitions, the designed landscape at Stowe eventually covered 10,000 acres – stretching a mile and a half wide and four miles from north to south.

Walpole later wrote of this forgotten hero that his 'many detached thoughts' marked the 'dawn of modern taste', for it was Bridgeman who first broke the bonds of all-out 17th-century formality. As the landscape at Stowe attests, his concern was for a sense of place and a vastness of scale. According to Peter Willis, the authority on Bridgeman, his style can be described as a mix of the traditional (parterres, avenues, geometric lakes), the transitional (garden buildings, lawns, and amphitheatre examples survive at both Cliveden and Claremont), and the progressive (rides and key vantage points). But without a doubt his single greatest contribution to the evolution of the landscape was the introduction of the 'ha-ha' (a sunken wall or hedge). Invisible to someone looking out over the landscape, but an effective barrier against livestock, this 'capital stroke, the leading step to all that has followed' enabled the surrounding 'cultivated fields, and even morsels of a forest appearance', or as it became known, the 'borrowed landscape' to be brought into focus and into the garden. And as Walpole triumphantly concluded, 'how rich, how gay, how picturesque the face of the country!'

Unlike Walpole, Bridgeman did not commit his theories to paper and as a man he is even more elusive. We know that he wed Sarah in 1717 and had seven children, with only four of them surviving. He seems to have been apolitical and non-sectarian; certainly he got on well with another Sarah, the notoriously difficult Duchess of Marlborough (at Blenheim), and this is itself a testament to his good nature, patience, tact and diplomacy. His election to St Luke's Club of Artists in 1726 suggests a circle of friends composed of gentleman art connoisseurs, artists, and literati, and his appointment as royal gardener to George II in 1728 certainly would not have happened without the favour of the king and his queen, Caroline – both of whom Bridgeman had worked for prior to the accession. Yet despite his high income he left relatively little to his wife Sarah in his will, which suggests he enjoyed an extravagant lifestyle.

Lord Cobham took a very 'hands on' approach to his 28-acre garden which, by 1724, was reputed to be 'the finest seat in England'. The next decade saw further expansion and Stowe's reputation was spread far and wide by Cobham's literary friends, who included the poet Alexander Pope. Pope waxed lyrical in 1731, observing 'If any thing under Paradise could set me beyond all Earthly Cogitations, Stowe might do it. It is much more beautiful than when I saw it before'.

By the time Pope's words were written, Cobham had brought in a new landscape designer, William Kent (1688–1748). To quote Walpole again, Kent was 'painter enough to taste the charms of landscape, bold and opinionative enough to dare and to dictate, and born with a genius to strike out a great system from the twilight of imperfect essays. He leaped the fence, and saw that *all nature was a garden* [my italics]. He felt the delicious contrast of hill and valley changing imperceptibly into each other, tasted the beauty of the gentle swell, or concave scoop and remarked how loose groves crowned an easy eminence with happy ornament.'

Kent was baptized in Bridlington, Yorkshire on New Year's Day 1686. Poorly educated, he began an apprenticeship as a coach and house painter. But then he got lucky: his talent was recognized by three local philanthropists who sponsored the young man to travel to Italy and study. Based in Rome from 1708 until 1719, Kent developed his talents for painting and architecture, and also his friendships with young grandees on their Grand Tour, a customary adventure for the independently wealthy. Upon his return to England Kent was invited by Lord Burlington, whom he had met in Italy in 1714, to reside at

Chiswick House in London. The pair became lifelong friends and Burlington introduced Kent into his circle, which included Pope and Walpole. Referred to affectionately as 'signor' or 'Kentino', he was considered quick-witted, amusing, and knowledgeable about all things Italian.

Kent worked by producing perspective drawings, but while he was a sublime theorist, practicalities were sadly not his strong point and his horticultural knowledge was lacking. The realities of translating his sketches into living landscape and picturesque buildings were left to horticulturists and craftsmen and, according to Dorothy Stroud, he also 'suffered from poor health, a tendency to indolence, and a strong dislike of travelling'. As a result, Cobham was one of relatively few patrons who were prepared to put up with Kent's idiosyncrasies and 'wait for his spasmodic visits and to sort out the muddles which frequently ensued through his inexplicit instructions'.

In the Eastern garden Cobham proudly chose to broadcast his Whiggish political ideals and morals through an extraordinary collection of buildings in different architectural styles, some by his favourite architect, James Gibb and others by William Kent. In keeping with Kent's vision, the landscape was pastoral although livestock was fenced in between the Gothic Temple, whose style symbolized ancient British liberties, and the Temple of Friendship, built for informal meetings of Cobham's all-male drinking and political clique. Egyptian, Greek, Roman and Gothic leitmotifs were all employed to illustrate Cobham's aspirations of liberty, empire, and moral and political instruction. Classical-style architecture, on the other hand, stood for the perceived parallel between the political make-up of the Roman Republic and the contemporary development of London. In the words of the 17th-century pantheist John Toland, London was considered 'a new Rome in the West' that 'could grasp at empire like Rome itself'.

But life in the garden wasn't all roses: in 1733 Cobham fell out with the Whig government over the Excise Bill and became leader of 'Cobham's Cubs' also known as the 'Boy Patriots' – a group of parliamentarian Whigs that opposed Sir Robert Walpole and believed his policies and corrupt Parliament were selling true Whig values down the river. This political epiphany is also reflected in the garden's iconography, for in Kent's Elysian Fields, facing the Temple of British Worthies but on the opposite bank of the River Styx, Cobham erected the Temple of Modern Virtue. Deliberately built as a ruin, it featured a headless statue, allegedly of Robert Walpole. By this time the physical construction of much of Kent's designs was being overseen by Lancelot Brown (later known as 'Capability' Brown). Kent had left Stowe in the mid-1730s for 'career reasons': now that Kent had ingratiated himself with George II he could not afford to be associated with Cobham, who was now rather antagonistic towards both Parliament and monarch.

Thanks to the plaudits of Alexander Pope and others, visiting Stowe became so popular that an inn was built near the estate gate to accommodate visitors and in 1744 Stowe became the first garden to publish a guidebook (which had reached its 16th edition by 1820). Lord Cobham died in 1749 and Brown departed to forge his career with private clients. Stowe passed to Cobham's nephew, Richard Grenville, a proud, quarrelsome and ambitious man who wasn't averse to using his political influence to secure honours and jobs, and didn't share Cobham's passion for making gardens. But Lord Cobham's contribution to English gardening is commemorated in 'Lord Cobham's Pillar', a tall octagonal tower designed by Brown for Lady Cobham in tribute to her husband. The sides are adorned with quotations, including verses by Pope in praise of Cobham's garden and, until lightning struck in 1957, Lord Cobham's statue, which gazed down proudly from above.

Westbury Court Garden, *GLOUCESTERSHIRE* *
MAYNARD COLCHESTER

The low, flat water meadows by the banks of the River Severn in Gloucestershire were perfectly suited to the formal Dutch garden style that came to Britain with the reign of William of Orange and his wife Mary, daughter of James II, between 1688 and 1702. Johannes Kip's bird's-eye view illustrations for Atkyns's *Ancient and Present State of Gloucestershire* (1712) depict over 20 variations on the Dutch garden theme; but today, Westbury Court is a rare survival.

Maynard Colchester (1664–1715) inherited Westbury Court in 1694 and gathered a fine collection of plants to complement his water garden. His inspiration to 'go Dutch' may have been his formidable neighbour, Catherine Boevey of Flaxley Abbey, the daughter of an Amsterdam merchant who maintained strong Dutch connections. Catherine certainly helped Maynard to co-found the Society for Promoting Christian Knowledge (SPCK) in 1698, which continues to be one of the greatest and most important societies within the Church of England to this day.

Colchester proudly began work on his impressive garden in 1696 with the creation of a long canal. Three years later he purchased a prickly collection of 1,000 three-year-old hollies, a number of similarly aged yews and a dozen standard hollies. At one end of the canal Colchester added a *clairvoyée* (an ornamental metal grille set in the wall to enable views out) and at the other he placed the Tall Pavilion. In 1702 came the arrival of '100 iris's 100 crocas 50 junquills 50 hyacynths double 50 double narcissus's 50 anenomys 50 ranunculus's 150 tulips and 1000 ews [yews]', a floral selection that reveals that planting was proceeding along Dutch lines. Colchester's nephew, another Maynard (1703–57), inherited the property in 1715 and added the T-shaped canal parallel to the original one, as well as a gazebo, statuary and a second clairvoyée. But fashions were changing fast and, when the younger Colchester died in 1748, the garden was considered so *passé* that it was abandoned and soon fell into disrepair. When the National Trust took over the estate in 1967 the garden infrastructure was in a desperate state and required major restoration. Thankfully, Kip's drawing of 1707 enabled the Trust to recreate part of the ornamental parterre; laid out with neatly clipped box hedges and filled with sparse plantings of botanical gems in the period style. The elder Colchester meticulously kept account books, which have enabled his passions for bulbs, flowers and trees to be brought back to life.

lust

'A *passionate desire* for something or someone.
A *sensuous appetite* regarded as sinful.'

A sunny summer's afternoon in a beautiful garden, the
sweet fragrance of flowers wafted on a gentle zephyr, the
soothing drone of bees, shade dappling the interior of a
secluded bower. What more could one want from a
location for a tryst? Certainly gardens have frequently
been used by lustful owners as the perfect 'mood setting'
environment in which to seduce and philander, but there
is far more to them than that. As with all the other
emotions discussed here, lust has found that gardens and
landscapes are the perfect stage for a great diversity of its
expression. From the straightforward – the hot-blooded,
randy dandy setting out to seduce a dairymaid, through
the blatant sexual iconography that leaves little to the
imagination to the subtle allegorical expression that
required deciphering, lustful intention is as varied as its
manifestation, its outcome as unpredictable as its purpose.

Blenheim Palace, *OXFORDSHIRE*
HENRY II & ROSAMOND CLIFFORD

Garden buildings, often with comfy couches and sometimes decorated with erotic murals, have provided intimate retreats for lovers and seducers for centuries. In one of the earliest examples of lust-inspired garden architecture Henry II (1133–1189) built 'Rosamond's Bower' within the grounds of Woodstock (now Blenheim) Palace in the 1100s. Reputedly located at the centre of a maze, and consisting of opulently furnished underground apartments with secret passages that led to the outside at some distance from the palace, Henry made it for his mistress, the fair Rosamond Clifford (c.1133–1179), and her children. The idea was that Henry could indulge his lustful love affair without the queen's knowledge and Rosamond and family could leave without being observed. It's rumoured, though not proven, that the queen discovered her husband's secret and, consumed with jealousy and hate, murdered her rival. In the age of chivalry this story of royal intrigue and passion quickly gained legendary status and a similar bower became a 'must have' garden feature for other members of the nobility.

Clevedon Court, *SOMERSET* *
WILLIAM MAKEPEACE THACKERAY

It was Oscar Wilde who wrote 'The book of life begins with a man and a woman in the garden', and down the centuries the garden has often been the setting for a display of lust and sexual innuendo, sexuality and sensuality, romance and love. An author whose tangled web of lust involved a real-life garden was William Makepeace Thackeray (1811–63).

Thackeray's wife Isabella suffered from mental illness and was 'confined'; she was looked after by a family in Essex, while his daughters lived with relatives

It was Oscar Wilde who wrote 'The book of life begins with a man and a woman in the garden'

in Paris. So in the 1840s William spent much of his time alone, often at Clevedon Court with his friend the Rev. William Henry Brookfield, as the guest of Sir Charles Elton. Brookfield was married to Jane Octavia, the daughter of the house but – somewhat unfortunately considering the circumstances – Thackeray fell in love with her. One day in 1848, while walking with Jane in the terraced garden for which Clevedon Court is renowned, he professed his passion. In return, Jane confided that her marriage was an unhappy one. Sadly, the course of their true love did not run smoothly and four years later their friendship ended – it seems likely that Jane's uncle-in-law, Henry Hallam, paid her an annuity as a bribe to make her break it off. Both Jane and William, her husband, are captured for posterity in Thackeray's novels. Jane appears as Amelia Sedley in *Vanity Fair* and Lady Castlewood in *Henry Esmond* and William is the model for the Rev. Charles Honeyman in *The Newcomers*.

Left: This portrait of William Makepeace Thackeray (1811–1863) by Sir Joseph Edgar Boehm hangs on the landing at Clevedon Court.

Cliveden, *BUCKINGHAMSHIRE* *
THE COUNTESS OF SHREWSBURY, 11TH EARL OF SHREWSBURY,
2ND DUKE OF BUCKINGHAM, JOHN PROFUMO, CHRISTINE KEELER

Cliveden has been the setting for more than a few lustful incidents over the years. At the more heartless end of the scale was Anna Brudenell, Countess of Shrewsbury (1642–1702), whose cold-blooded actions are immortalized in a flowerbed shaped like a rapier, bearing the date 1668. It commemorates the duel fought between her cuckolded husband, Francis Talbot, 11th Earl of Shrewsbury (1623–68), and her lover, George Villiers, 2nd Duke of Buckingham (1628–87). An account of the event was recorded by the ever-salacious diarist, Samuel Pepys:

> 'they met yesterday in a close near Barne Elmes (near Putney, London) and there fought; and my Lord Shrewsbury is run through the body from the right breast through the shoulder, and Sir J. Talbot all along up one of his arms and Jenkins killed upon the place [Talbot and Jenkins were the Earl's seconds] ... This will make the world think that the King hath good councillors about him, when the Duke of Buckingham, the greatest man about him, is a fellow of no more Sobriety than to fight about a whore.'

Pepys certainly had a way with words. Shrewsbury was mortally wounded, since Buckingham had ignored the accepted etiquette by running him through the body. And tradition has it that Anna, dressed as Buckingham's page, watched her husband being killed without emotion. Certainly she was capable of such callousness since, on an earlier occasion, she had personally orchestrated a near fatal attack on her former lover, Harry Killigrew, during which his servant was killed. She and Buckingham were well-matched: he was also an all-round nasty piece of work, renowned for his lack of principles and his quarrelsome temper. He has been described as 'a politician, diplomat, poet, playwright, amateur chemist, gambler, adulterer and murderer'.

In more recent times, Cliveden was the setting for a less violent, but just as scandalous, scene of lust and poor judgement. For it was around the swimming pool at Cliveden, on 8 July 1961, that John Profumo (1915–2006) – a house guest and close friend of the owner, Lord Astor – first encountered a young, naked and dripping wet Christine Keeler (b.1942). The Conservative Minister for War and the beautiful 19-year-old model-cum-topless showgirl quickly developed what Keeler later described as 'a very well mannered screw of convenience; only in other people's minds, much later, was it "An Affair"' (she was also sleeping with Yevgeny 'Eugene' Ivanov, a supposed Russian spy, at the time). When Profumo lied about his involvement with Keeler to the House of Commons in March 1963, he sealed his fate and threw away his political career. By today's standards the 'Profumo Affair' seems relatively tame, although it was one of the first times that the press published a scandalous story about an 'establishment' figure. Thus it helped set the trend for the scandals that so suffice the tabloids of today.

Clumber Park, *NOTTINGHAMSHIRE* *
ROBERT THOROTON

Classical mythology abounds with tales of passion and love played out in sylvan settings. Robert Thoroton (1623–78), whose *History of Nottinghamshire* was republished in expanded form by John Throsby in 1790, wistfully acknowledges that his days of lustful thoughts are long gone, but describes Clumber Park as the perfect romantic setting for young passion:

> 'At an age when men in general are not enamoured with a looking back on their youthful years, I could not help indulging an innocent thought, that these were the sweetest love walks I had ever seen; here youth, beauty and innocence might solace in a reciprocal exchange of vows and sentiments, in uninterrupted retirement; silent as the grave, except from the melody of the little warbling foresters and the bleating, at intervals, of the playful lambkins.'

Garden designers and artists alike were quick to see the erotic powers of the garden, as a place where normal social constraints could be thrown to the wind.

... the erotic powers of the garden ... a place where normal social constraints could be thrown to the wind

Eywood, *HEREFORDSHIRE*
COUNT TELEKI, MISS BICKERSTETH

The 'only daughter and heiress' was a particularly troublesome breed in matters of the heart or, not to put too fine a point on it, lust. Such innocent young ladies were easy prey for a particular brand of dirty rotten scoundrel – the fortune hunter – for whom the love of Mammon was the real passion. In some cases the 'spoilt brat' of a daughter wilfully hoisted her own petard, but at other times the doting parents were at fault. According to the September 1852 diary of Mary Elizabeth Lucy, of Charlecote Park in Warwickshire, an unfortunate train of events was set in motion during her visit to Lord and Lady Langdale at Eywood, where another guest was the Hungarian Count Teleki. One afternoon, taking a long walk in the park, the party came upon a ditch. She recounts what ensued as follows:

'we jumped over, except Miss Bickersteth (the Langdales's only child and heir) who declared she could not possibly jump it, when Count Teleki – more gallant than even Sir Walter Raleigh of old – lay down and, stretching himself full length across the ditch, bid Miss Bickersteth make a bridge of him, which she did and stepped over his back and we all screamed with laughing.'

The 'only daughter and heiress' was a particularly troublesome breed in matters of the heart or, not to put too fine a point on it, lust

When Mary Elizabeth told Lady Langdale she was sure the Count had an eye for the latter's daughter, the good lady replied with the vapidity reserved for doting parents:

'Oh! No, you are mistaken, he would not presume to think of such a thing, he is only a poor exile and his whole heart and mind are given to his unhappy country, but we are very fond of him, and he is teaching us Hungarian.'

But Mary Elizabeth was right in her suspicions that there was more than language lessons on the agenda:

'I thought to myself, you blind mother, your eyes will be opened when it is too late and so it came to pass for as soon as her daughter came of age she married him and the wicked Count (for he was wicked) when he found that her fortune was strictly settled so that he could not spend it, he wished her goodbye three days after her wedding, saying he had a wife and a large family in Hungary. She never saw him again and died a miserable woman not many years afterwards.'

Gibside, *NORTHUMBERLAND* *
MARY ELEANOR BOWES, JOHN BOWES-LYON

The wilful Mary Eleanor (1749–1800) was the only child of George Bowes (1701–60). Bowes, who had been a mix of hot-headed youth, shrewd businessman and intellectual patron of the arts, transformed the garden at Gibside with money he made from coal. However, her father's house and legacy of £600,000 brought nothing but grief, for Mary Eleanor proved to be particularly inept in her selection of partners. Her first husband, whom she wed on her 18th birthday in a £3,000 dress, was John Lyon, 9th Earl of Strathmore (1737–76) who, in accordance with George's wishes, changed his name to Bowes-Lyon, and was thus an ancestor of Queen Elizabeth, the late Queen Mother. In 1776, after nine years of unhappy marriage, John died of consumption.

Mary Eleanor purchased Stanley House near the Chelsea Physic garden in London and proceeded to build greenhouses and conservatories, filling them with exotic plants from South Africa. Such was her plant knowledge that Jesee Foot, the family doctor, said she was 'the most intelligent female botanist of the age'. However, she did not show the same level of intelligence in love for, rather than enjoy her freedom, Mary Eleanor became pregnant by her lover George Grey (who was generally considered to be a decent chap), but dumped him to gallop headlong into an awful liaison with Andrew Robinson Stoney. An Irish rake, on whom Thackeray based the main character of his novel *The Memoirs of Barry Lyndon*, Robinson Stoney treated his wife most cruelly for eight years. Eventually, in February 1785, Mary Eleanor fled and sued for divorce, citing her husband's repeated adultery. In desperation, Eleanor threw herself into developing, creating (among other features) a 'greenhouse' (orangery to most people), which was an ornate pile with Tuscan columns and tall sash windows in which she indulged in her passion for collecting exotic plants. Facing bankruptcy, Stoney-Bowes (he also changed his name) arranged for Mary Eleanor's kidnap and, literally holding a gun to her head, ordered her to drop the divorce suit – but she refused. Eventually, Mary Eleanor (later dubbed 'The Unhappy Countess') was released unharmed and Stoney-Bowes was captured, convicted in London, and imprisoned. This time, Mary Eleanor had learnt her lesson and spent the rest of her life single – while her ex gave the English language the term 'stoney broke'.

Osterley Park, *MIDDLESEX* *
SARAH ANN CHILD, 10TH EARL OF WESTMORLAND

Lustful behaviour can lead to dire consequences, as Sarah Ann Child (b.1765), eldest child of wealthy banker Robert Child discovered, literally to her cost. Osterley was Robert's pride and joy, and, with the aid of architect Robert Adam, he completely refurbished both house and grounds from 1761–80. Although the designer is unknown, the grounds were famed for their serpentine lakes and for a menagerie housing rare and exotic birds. If things had gone to plan, it could all have been Sarah's.

In May 1782 the impetuous 17-year-old Sarah became smitten with the dashing but impoverished John Fane, 10th Earl of Westmorland (1759–1841), popularly known as 'Rapid'. Apparently, knowing her father would never agree to the union, John sneakily asked Robert Child in casual conversation what *he* would do, speaking hypothetically, if he was in love with a girl whose father didn't approve of the match. Given the situation, Robert was said to have thoughtlessly answered 'elope, of course'. Unfortunately for Robert, that's exactly what the young lovers then did, absconding to Gretna Green. In the 18th-century equivalent of a high-speed car chase, they were nearly thwarted by Child's pursuing servants, only escaping when John shot one of the horses, at Sarah's urging. The couple were wed and Sarah's father seemed somewhat reconciled to the fact. But, alas, he did harbour a lasting resentment – and was determined that his estate should not go to the Westmorland family. When Robert died two months later he left his fortune – which included both Osterley Park and Upton House, in Warwickshire – to his wife, then to his daughter's second child (another Sarah), thereby preventing it going to the Westmorland family although on condition that the future heir was to 'take and use upon all occasions the name of Child only'.

Stourhead, *WILTSHIRE* *
HENRY HOARE II

Many a stately garden is adorned with lust-inspired ornamentation, be it a conventional statue of Venus, Aphrodite or Eros, or a more unconventional piece of trim topiary – such as the carefully clipped box hedging at Nymans in West Sussex, reputedly representing Shirley Bassey's shapely buttocks. But perhaps the most sublime sculptural expression of sensuality is the 'Nymph of the Grot' who reclines languidly inside the circular domed chamber of the grotto at Stourhead. Within her shady stone bower, lined with limestone imported from Italy, she is raised on a dais in the middle of a crystal clear pool, illuminated from above by a ray of light. A beautiful and voluptuous water nymph, she is carved from the whitest marble and styled in imitation of the statue of Adriane in the Vatican Belvedere Gardens. So she conveys both a nymph's erotic sexuality and a rather more earthy link with fecundity, since Adriane's husband was Dionysus, God of Fertility.

Stowe Landscape Gardens, *BUCKINGHAMSHIRE* *
LORD COBHAM, WILLIAM KENT, SIR JOHN VANBRUGH, CONWAY RAND

Lord Cobham, who began what became a massive garden in the 1700s, clearly took pleasure in the physical manifestation of the family motto *Templa Quam Dilecta* ('how beautiful are thy temples'), also a pun on the family name, Temple. Cobham's remodelling of the grounds incorporated over 40 temples, monuments and other secret corners. All these garden buildings were devised to have hidden meanings or symbolism and it's likely that he devised this complex iconography with the help of his garden designers – Charles Bridgeman and, later, William Kent, his literary friends and his nephew, the poet Gilbert West. Experts have expended much time on examining the significance of Cobham's complex design and have come to the conclusion that the Western and Eastern gardens represent the Choice of Hercules, a popular allegorical theme in the 18th century. Essentially, Hercules faced the difficult decision between taking the path of virtue or that of vice (naturally, each choice was offered to him by a beautiful and alluring woman). The visitor to Stowe was offered the same choice by choosing to visit the Eastern Garden, which Cobham used to state his political affiliation and allegiance (see Stowe, page 49), or the Western Garden, replete with themes of unrequited love and profane love, suggestive inscriptions and erotic murals inside various garden buildings.

Much of the evidence for the Western garden's meaning comes from Gilbert West's poem 'Stowe' composed in 1732. While the eye would have marvelled at the manipulated landscape and decorated garden buildings, the sexual iconography was designed not to celebrate bodily pleasures but to stir depressing, lovelorn emotions. For example, the Lake Pavilions, a series of graceful porticos built to Sir John Vanbrugh's design, dealt with unrequited love – the rear walls were painted with the stories taken from Guarini's opera *Il Pastor Fido*, featuring unhappy lovers Dorinda and Sylvio, and Myrtillo and Amaryllis. Introducing the subject of unfaithful love, the exterior of William Kent's Temple of Venus was ornamented by statues of the most notorious adulteresses in history – Cleopatra and Faustina (daughter of Roman Emperor Antoninus, noted for her fondness for sailors and gladiators). Inside the temple Kent warmed to his theme: inspired by Spenser's *Faerie Queene*, he included highly explicit murals by Francesco Sleter, telling the tale of Malbecco and Hellenore, the latter cavorting with well-endowed satyrs. The Rev. John Wesley, who visited in 1779, disapproved of the paintings greatly, calling them 'lewd' and 'neither well designed nor executed' (though it seems he must have inspected them closely to be able to comment!). Here too, as in the 'sleeping parlour' nearby, was a 'pleasuring sopha' (sofa), perhaps intended for the comfort of visiting couples 'inspired' by the artworks, with a Latin inscription that translates as:

'Let him love, who never loved before;
Let him who always lov'd, now love the more.'

To leave the visitor in no doubt as to the lustful intent of the symbolism, the Artificial Ruins at the head of the lake house statues of three satyrs and a dancing Venus while the 'Rotondo', originally named the Temple of Venus, contains a gilded Venus de Medici; and then, to top it all, the spurting Obelisk in the Octagon Lake – so, some none-too-subtle reminders of female and male lust. This part of the garden is also the site of the Private Grotto, which West later dubbed the 'Randibus', as it was here, reputedly, that the vicar of Stowe, Conway Rand pursued and then sexually assaulted a 'frightened maid' from the house. West got it all down in rather salacious verse:

'A Private Grotto promis'd safe Retreat:
Alas! too private, for too safely there
The fierce Pursuer seiz'd the helpless Fair;
The Fair he seiz'd, while round him all the

Throng Of laughing Dryads, Hymenaeals sung:
Pronubial Juno gave the mystick Sign,
And Venus nodded from her neighb'ring Shrine [the Rotondo].'

Understandably perhaps, the grotto was subsequently renamed 'Dido's Cave', with the association with hopeless love – the tragic queen committed suicide when her paramour Aeneas left Carthage to found Rome – suitably depicted in a painting that was added in 1738, along with an appropriate inscription from Virgil.

If that hadn't dampened the visitor's lustful ardour, they could repair to the Cave of St Augustine, a root house hidden in the wood behind the Temple of Bacchus (dedicated to the God of lechery, drunkenness and wine) which boasted some smutty verse, probably by Richard Glover. Based on some of the more bawdy passages from the 'Confessions of St Augustine', this ribaldry graphically described the problems of celibate monastic life and some of the 'self-inflicted' cures, which included the rather impractical decision by Augustine to make himself a woman of snow to satisfy his lust: she was doomed to melt in the heat of passion. And, just to rub it in, the inscription on the Pyramid reminded the aging male of his physical and, by association, sexual decrepitude. Translated from the Latin, it reads:

'You have played enough, eaten enough, and drunk enough,
Now it is time to leave the stage for younger men
Lest youth this selfish love of life condemn
And hiss thee from a scene designed for them'

Indeed, the garden iconography at Stowe is all about men, with the Western Garden being a somewhat misogynistic landscape: the women represented are temptresses or adulteresses, encouraging poor men to commit lustful acts against their will. Conversely, the path of virtue in the Eastern Garden is a male dominated realm, where all the females present – Nike, the Goddess of Victory, the Muses, and Elizabeth I –

are there to inspire or celebrate male achievements, or to be praised for their man-like qualities.

West Wycombe Park* and Medmenham Abbey, *BUCKINGHAMSHIRE*
SIR FRANCIS DASHWOOD

Created by Sir Francis Dashwood (1708–81), West Wycombe was certainly *the* 18th century's most licentious and libidinous landscapes. When Lord Esher, the then Chairman of the Historic Buildings Committee accepted the property on behalf of the National Trust in 1944, he said 'It gives me great pleasure to accept this ancient house of vice, or rather I should say, this house of ancient vice'. Certainly there was nothing unrequited, jealous, or celibate about this garden. On the contrary, it was earthy and pithy, and celebrated sex and the female form as sensuous, erotic, and pleasurable.

Much about the colourful life of its creator, Lord le Despencer, alias Sir Francis Dashwood, 2nd Baron of West Wycombe, is the stuff of legend. Born in 1708 into an illustrious line of turkey merchants, he was part of a family that had raised itself to the aristocracy by sheer hard work. According to Sir Horace Walpole he was a man with 'a coarse blunt manner', 'notorious for singing profane and lewd catches', with 'the staying power of a stallion and the impetuosity of a bull'. Certainly Dashwood was a 'larger than life' character – an iconoclast with a needle-sharp sense of humour and a libidinous, devil-may-care streak at least a mile wide. And it is for his libertine, rakish behaviour that he is most remembered. He happened to be in Rome in 1730 when the death of Pope Clement XII was announced and immediately set about staging a mock papal election. Another such merry jape was described by the ubiquitous Walpole:

> 'It was on Good Friday when each person who attends the service in the Sistine Chapel, as he enters takes a small scourge from an attendant at the door. The chapel is dimly lighted and there are three

candles which are extinguished by the priest one by one: at the putting out of the first, the penitents take off one part of their dress; at the next, still more; and in the darkness which follows the extinguishing of the third candle, lay on their shoulders with groans and lamentations. Sir Francis Dashwood thinking this mere stage effect, entered with others dressed in a large watchman's coat, demurely he took his scourge from the priest and advanced to the end of the chapel, where, on the darkness ensuing, he drew from beneath his coat an English horsewhip and flogged right and left quite down the chapel and made his escape, the congregation exclaiming "Il Diavolo! Il Diavolo!" thinking the evil one was upon them with a vengeance. The consequences of this frolic might have been serious to him, had he not immediately left the Papal dominions.'

Dashwood's questionable sense of fun came to the fore again when he travelled to St Petersburg with Lord Forbes, and reputedly seduced the Empress Anna of Russia by dressing up as King Charles XII of Sweden (who was already dead at the time). Fortunately his antics didn't prevent the establishment of an Anglo-Russian Commercial Treaty, the intended reason for Forbes' visit.

But there is no denying that Dashwood was also intelligent, cultured, and well-travelled; he was passionate about the arts and in particular architecture. He was also mindful of the disadvantaged and served from 1741 as the MP for New Romney, introducing a Poor Relief Bill in 1747 and rising to Lord Chancellor in Lord Bute's ill-fated ministry. And he was not above self-criticism, considering himself 'the worst Chancellor of the Exchequer that ever appeared'. A perplexing character, it's perhaps surprising to find that Dashwood was also a practising Christian, a friend of John Wesley and, later in life, with the aid of another friend Benjamin Franklin (both were postmaster-generals of their respective countries), author of an abridged version of the *Book of Common Prayer* (1773), which, while it received approbation in America, was rejected in England.

Above: The north front of the house, viewed from across the lake with a wooden bridge and the rotondo, 1751–3. Painted by William Flannan and hung in West Wycombe.

When it came to gardens, Dashwood – like Lord Cobham at Stowe – was keen on populating the landscape with interesting buildings. But Dashwood's intentions were somewhat less subtle: rather than admonishing the lustful visitor, he wanted to create places for him and his friends to have a rollicking good time. Dashwood was a great one for creating clubs of like-minded people, who shared his love of culture and good living. In 1732 he established the Society of Dilettanti. Despite Walpole's rather disdainful comment (he had not been asked to join!) that it was 'a club for which the nominal qualification is having been in Italy and the real one, being drunk: the two chiefs are Lord Middlesex and Sir Francis Dashwood, who were seldom sober the whole time they were in Italy', the society sought to actively promote an awareness and appreciation of classical art. It also funded excavations at Herculaneum (1738) and Pompeii (1748), and the study tour undertaken by James 'Athenian' Stuart and Nicholas Revett to Athens in 1751, resulting in the publication of the influential *Antiquities of Athens* (1762) and *Ionia* (1769). It was this last expedition that inspired Dashwood to erect the Temple of the Winds at West Wycombe in 1759 (another was built in the lake at Shugborough in Staffordshire, the residence of Thomas Anson, 1st Lord Lichfield, a founding member of the Dilettanti).

Rather less academic was Dashwood's Divan Club, whose members dressed up as Sultans (and Sultanas) and revelled in the worship of Bacchus. Lust was certainly on the menu there and even more so in his most notorious creation in about 1750 – the Society (or Knights) of St Francis of Wycombe, also called the Monks of Medmenham, but now better remembered as the Hellfire Club (although it was not called by that name during its existence). This club was essentially a group of powerful friends who shared Dashwood's love of revelry and his lustful appetites – described by one initiate as a 'set of worthy, jolly fellows, happy disciples of Venus and Bacchus, (who) got together occasionally to celebrate woman in wine and to give more zest to the festive meeting, they plucked every luxurious idea from the ancients and enriched their own modern pleasures with the tradition of classic luxury.' The pretence of being a mock religious order may have been a dig at Stowe and its owner Lord Cobham's moral concerns with celibacy – unquestionably, celibacy was not part of the doctrine of the so-called 'brotherhood'. Or perhaps the inspiration was Rabelais' fictional Abbey of Theleme, whose motto, '*Fay ce que voudras*' ('Do as you wish'), was inscribed above the entrance to the Society's 'retreat' – which was often thought to be the Hellfire Caves at West Wycombe. These natural caves were excavated in 1750–2 by Dashwood as a way to provide work for unemployed farm workers and then restored, fronted with a mock-ruin of a church in flint. But, being 91 metres

(300 feet) underground and rather damp and, given Dashwood's love of comfort, it seems unlikely to have been the venue for regular meetings. Most of Dashwood's more licentious goings-on took place at Medmenham Abbey, a nearby ruin that he kitted out in opulent style.

What little we know about the activities of Dashwood and his monks comes mostly from John Wilkes, an erstwhile member, or 'fallen brother', who published his *Description of Medmenham Abbey* as a note to Charles Churchill's poem *The Candidate* in 1764. As a deliberately biased account of the society's activities, it was designed to embarrass his previous host, who was indeed forced to dismantle Medmenham in 1766. It is evident that proceedings were overseen by Dashwood as Prior, and that there were many illustrious members, including Frederick, Prince of Wales; John Stuart, 3rd Earl of Bute; George Bubb Doddington (later Lord Melcombe Regis); the Duke of Queensberry; Sir Henry Vansittart; the satirist George Selwyn; painter William Hogarth; poets Robert Lloyd and Charles Churchill; and MPs John Tucker and Thomas Potter (the son of a former Archbishop of Canterbury). There was an inner core of 12 'apostles' who attended regularly, while the full membership gathered for weekend meetings three times a year. An 'abbot' was appointed annually to organize activities – one of his perks being that he also had first pick of the women.

Stories about the various activities that took place have been wildly exaggerated, but the 'monks' certainly did indulge in all sorts of pleasures, including dressing up and acting out mock-religious ceremonies, the consumption of good food and wine (drunk from silver goblets shaped like women's breasts), and free love. The female contingent was most probably London prostitutes, although certain 'society' ladies, including Lady Mary Montagu Wortley, the mother-in-law of Lord Bute, were rumoured to have participated in the fun. The décor at Medmenham was in keeping with their recreations and the building had a well-stocked cellar, a library of pornography, board games, musical instruments and a boat for fishing (though one doubts if there was much time for the latter). And the abbey gardens didn't escape from all this lust and abandon. With candid inscriptions and graphic sculpture, they made no attempt to conceal the kind of 'worship' Dashwood and pals were enjoying. As related by Wilkes, at the centre of the orchard was 'a very grotesque figure, and in his hand a reed stood flaming, tipt with fire, to use Milton's words: and you might trace out PENI TENTO non PENITENTI'. This was most likely a statue of Priapus (the son of Venus and Bacchus) boasting a large and erect penis (hence the pun in the inscription). Another statue, of Venus stooping to pull a thorn out of her foot, stood at the entrance to a grotto:

> 'The statue turned from you, and just over the two nether hills of snow (her buttocks) were these lines of Virgil: "here is the place where the way divided in two: this on the right is our route to Heaven; but the left-hand path exacts punishment from the wicked, and sends them to pitiless Hell". Inside, over a mossy couch, was the following exhortation: (trans. from Virgil) "Go into action, you youngsters; put everything you've got into it together, both of you; let not doves outdo your cooings, not ivy your embraces, nor oysters your kisses".'

Surely there's a parody here, of the gardens at Stowe – where Lord Cobham's Western and Eastern gardens represented vice and virtue, respectively? The reference to the statue of Venus recalls Stowe's Venus, and the mossy couch is probably a dig at the 'pleasuring sopha' in Stowe's Temple of Venus.

Dashwood made more references to nearby Stowe on making his garden at West Wycombe itself, which he began in about 1735, although, progress was interrupted by his travels to Europe and possibly North Africa. Work only began in earnest in 1745, when Sir Frances wed Sarah Ellys, whose dowry paid for much of the garden work. But marriage hadn't mended Dashwood's lustful ways: that same year, his good friend

Bubb Doddington teased him for being 'like a Publick Reservoir … laying your Cock in every private Family that has any place fitt to receive it'. Fifteen years later, it was Doddington's specific bequest of £500 to build 'an Arch Temple Column or Additional Room to such of his Seats where it is likely to remain the longest as a Testimony to after Times of my Affection and Gratitude for the Invariable and very endearing Friendship he has honoured me with' that inspired Dashwood to erect the Mausoleum in West Wycombe's grounds.

The Mausoleum was not only a monument to his friend, but to Dashwood's own dedication to the theatrical and to extravagant sexual excess. Inside, murals on the ceilings depicted the wedding of Ariadne and Bacchus. Outside, rather than cast pleasure and lust as vices as Cobham had done, Dashwood chose to celebrate both. The lake is shaped like a swan, which happens to be the county symbol of Buckinghamshire but was more likely a reference to the myth of Leda, who was ravished by Zeus in this form. *The Victoria County History, Buckinghamshire* vol. III tartly describes the landscape as 'laid out by a curious arrangement of streams, bushes and plantation to represent the female form.' Daniel P. Mannix, in his book *The Hellfire Club*, is more explicit: he describes how two mounds, each topped with a circle of red flowering plants, were lined up at a certain distance from a triangle of dark shrubbery. Sir Francis allegedly took a local priest up the church tower and, as he asked him what he thought of his garden, three fountains were turned on. Two of them spouted a milky white fluid from the top of each red flowered mound while the third gushed from the area of the shrubbery.

But this wanton display was beaten hands down by the most notorious garden feature at West Wycombe and perhaps in the history of English garden making – Dashwood's Venus' Temple and Parlour complex. Created between 1745–8 by John Donowell, the temple (whose domed roof has its own breast-like quality) housed a gilded replica of the statue of the Venus de Medici (as at Stowe), while the hill on which the Temple stands represented a *mons veneris* – the 'hill of venus', or female vulva. Below this, at ground level, is Venus' Parlour – an oval opening into a dark cave, flanked by curving screen walls that represent a pair of legs akimbo. The garden visitor was left in no doubt that this is a graphic representation of a vagina but, in case further confirmation was needed, over the entrance hovers a statue of Mercury – purported to be the god that conducted the souls of men to Paradise, but possibly also a pun on the contemporary cure for syphilis.

In May 1763 – the month after Lord Bute had resigned as Prime Minister, to be succeeded by George Grenville, younger brother of Stowe's owner, Richard – John Wilkes published another malicious article, this time in the *Public Advertiser*. He described this area of Dashwood's garden as 'the New Foundling hospital for wit' and ridicules Venus' Parlour, which he said was dedicated to:

'the Egyptian Hieroglyphic for ****. To this object his Lordship's devotion is undoubtedly sincere, though I believe it now not fervent, nor do I take him to be often prostrate, or indeed in any way regular in his ejaculations … As to the temple I have mentioned; you find at first what is called an error in limine for the Entrance to it is the same Entrance by which we all come into the world; and the door is what some idle wits have called the *Door of Life* … there are in these gardens no busts of Socrates, Epaminondas or Hampden; but there is a most indecent statue of the unnatural satyr'

The latter part of Wilkes's invective is a sneering comparison with Stowe, which, with its redeeming path of virtue imagery, he considered to be morally superior. Wilkes' tirade was part personal attack on Dashwood, part flattery of Richard Grenville, Wilkes' political ally and no friend of Lord Bute. To be even more inflammatory, Wilkes went on to suggest that Lord Bute – who was rumoured to be the lover of George III's mother – had recommended the construction of 'an

Erection, in a Paphian Column to stand at the Entrance (to Venus' Parlour) ... to be made of Scottish pebbles'. There is no evidence that it was ever built.

Dashwood's wife died in 1769, but he continued to live life to the full and to enjoy West Wycombe and its gardens, making changes to the house and enlarging the park from 1770 until his death in 1781. In 1774 the 66-year-old became father to Rachel Frances Antonia, by his mistress Frances Barry, and received another dubious accolade as the 'most careless and perhaps the most facetious libertine of his age'. On his death he was buried, appropriately, in the Mausoleum where his epitaph piously proclaims that he was 'Revered, Respected and beloved by all who knew him'. West Wycombe passed to his half-brother Sir John Dashwood King, who did little to the grounds. However, by the late 18th century the garden was considered to be like an 'over adorned foreign trollop, superficial and artificial, showy, useless, grotesque, excessive and unduly erotic'. The great landscape designer Humphry Repton made minor alterations under the direction of the second Sir John in 1793, and the Temple of Venus was demolished in 1819 on moral grounds.

The spirited 11th Baronet – another Francis – rebuilt the Temple of Venus in 1982, and it is reassuring to know that Sir Francis's descendants inherited some of his lust for life. In 1986 Sir Francis Dashwood's namesake hosted a fund-raising fête for the National Trust in the grounds, and reputedly planned – as one of the appropriate highlights – to present a staging of the Birth of Venus. This was to feature a beautiful young girl dressed only in a transparent bodystocking, arising from the waters of the lake in a shell. But the prudish 'powers that be' considered this prospect far too risqué and insisted the girl put on more clothes. In spite of this, Sir Francis allegedly organized a private viewing for his friends and guests, the night before: in true Dashwood style, it became known as the 'Undress Rehearsal'.

love

'An *intense* feeling of *deep affection.*
A *great interest and pleasure in something.*'

Love is a mighty powerful emotion and can be a great
source of strength and joy as well as sorrow and angst.
Moreover, devotion can take many forms, for example,
to a person, a place, a family, a religion and, particularly
in the case of the British, animals and gardens. Thus,
although gardens are passive in themselves, they are both
the source of great pleasure for those who invest so much
love and care in them, and simultaneously offer an arena
in which love can be displayed to others.

Baddesley Clinton, *WARWICKSHIRE* *
LADY CHATTERTON, EDWARD HENEAGE DERING,
MARMION EDWARD FERRERS, REBECCA DULCIBELLA ORPEN

In 1859, Georgiana, Lady Chatterton married Edward Heneage
Dering, a man 20 years her junior. A decade later the couple moved
into Baddesley Clinton in the forest of Arden with another couple,
Georgiana's nephew, Marmion Edward Ferrers, and his wife, Rebecca
Dulcibella Orpen. The foursome, staunch Catholics, spent their time
and a great deal of Edward's money reviving the estate, for although
Marmion was the one to inherit the property, he was penniless. But he
was 'the pleasantest and most genial of men', and evidently big-
hearted, if not rich: one day coming across an old lady stealing
firewood from the estate, rather than a reprimand, he carried the wood
home for her. He was also, it seems, simply big; when he caught three
poachers red-handed he dispensed his own punishment and 'floored
two of them (then) let them all go'.

Following the deaths of Georgiana (1876) and Marmion (1884), Rebecca and Edward married in 1885. Later on, in the 1940s, Undine Ferres ripped out many of the foursome's shrubbery plantings, which in good Victorian style contained much Portugal laurel and yew. Undine particularly disliked all that dark foliage, believing it to represent 'the dark forces of Catholicism'!

Canons Ashby, *NORTHAMPTONSHIRE* *
THE DRYDEN FAMILY, GEORGE LONDON, HENRY WISE

The Dryden family built the manor house in the 1550s acquiring the land after Henry VIII's dissolution of the monasteries – but the formal garden was first developed in the early 1700s by Edward Dryden (d.1717), who had amassed a fortune as a grocer and inherited the estate by a rather tortuous route. When John Dryden inherited Canons Ashby in the late 1600s, his direct heir, another John, was disinherited because he had run off with the steward's daughter. Another possible candidate, Erasmus Henry (son of the Poet Laureate, John Dryden), could not inherit without paying a prohibitive fine, because he was a Catholic who had served in the Papal Guard in Rome. In the end, the estate went to Edward, who immediately invited Erasmus to come and live with him. In the 1880s it was the wont of Sir Henry Dryden, archaeologist and antiquarian, to roam the roads about the estate dressed as a tramp. Accosting wayfarers he would tell them where a good meal was to be found, before leading his unsuspecting guests back to the house. There he would entertain them in the great mediaeval kitchen, plying them with his home brewed beer spiked with bicarbonate of soda for 'extra fizz'. The Dryden family were an illustrious bunch and are distant ancestors of Thomas Jefferson, George W. Bush and the late Diana, Princess of Wales.

Edward created his garden from 1708, continuing until his death in 1717. Calling on George London (d.1714) and Henry Wise

(1653–1738) of the famous Brompton Park Nursery in Kensington, London, he installed a series of descending terraces which survive intact as a rare example of their French-inspired style.

The Brompton Park Nursery had been co-founded in 1681 by London (the site is now underneath the South Kensington museums), who was joined there by Wise seven years later. For the next 25 years they were the pre-eminent garden designers of the day, erecting terraces and laying out parterres, digging canals and installing fountains, planting topiary, avenues, groves, wildernesses, bulbs and shrubs, all of which were supplied by the nursery. In fact they were so prolific that contemporary garden designer Switzer (who had been trained by them) wrote: 'The planting and raising of all sorts of trees is so much due to this undertaking 'twill be hard for any of posterity to lay their hands on a tree in any of these kingdoms that have not been a part of their care.'

Wise and London's layouts were vast, formal, and formulaic, influenced by the French Baroque style. London was appointed Royal Gardener to William III (1650–1702) in 1688, but was promptly sacked by Anne (1665–1714), when she became Queen in 1702, despite assisting her flight from the capital during the Glorious Revolution of 1688. She replaced him with Wise and simultaneously cut the budget for royal gardening. She later turned up her nose at William's intricate and extensive parterres at Hampton Court, having them grubbed out because she did not like the smell of the box hedging! Luckily, Edward Dryden was a far more sensitive and enthusiastic garden-lover and London and Wise were able to design a lovely romantic garden, with beautiful avenues leading to the lake, park and the church.

Right: Sir Henry Dryden, 4th Baronet (d.1899), photographed by Sir Arthur Dryden on the steps of Canons Ashby.

Chartwell, *KENT* *
SIR WINSTON CHURCHILL

Winston Churchill (1874–1965) loved his country home and once wrote to his beloved wife, Clemmie, 'I think it is very important to have animals, flowers and plants in one's life while it lasts'. He certainly loved animals: at Chartwell he kept a leopard, black swans from Australia and a Canada goose that followed him around the garden like a pet dog. He devotedly raised butterflies from larvae in the summerhouse and was very fond of his ornamental fish (see Chartwell, page 112).

Set within its sheltered valley and enjoying magnificent views out over the Weald of Kent, Churchill had been besotted by Chartwell at first sight. But, when it came on the market in 1921, he could not afford the £6,500 asking price. A year on his circumstances had changed, and he picked up the house and surrounding 80 acres for £5,000, later stating 'I bought Chartwell for the view'. Over the coming years Chartwell became the canvas for his garden-making, the muse for his paintings, a calming retreat from the hurly-burly of political life when in office and a private oasis when he was lost in the political desert. And, perhaps most importantly, it was a very happy family home and an idyllic place in which Winston and Clemmie lovingly raised their four children – Diana, Randolph, Sarah and Mary.

Winston Churchill: 'I think it is very important to have animals, flowers and plants in one's life while it lasts'

Churchill certainly added his own particular flavour to fathering – fond of imitating a gorilla, he used to chase the children round the garden and he also built for them a little brick summer-house and a two-storey tree-house that was 20 feet up one of the two huge lime trees on the Entrance Lawn. On one occasion Sarah found her cousin Peregrine subdividing the tree-house into two rooms. Asking why, she was treated to a truly Churchillian response: 'This is my study, there are times when men have to be alone'.

The great man spent the summers of 1924 and 1925 happily digging his new lake and Lees-Milne recalled 'Mr C., clad in waders, standing up to his chest in mud and shouting directions like Napoleon before Austerlitz'. Indeed, Winnie was apparently never happier than when 'wallowing in the most filthy black mud you ever saw, with the vilest odour'. He personally built most of the vegetable garden walls and became so adept a 'brickie', laying about 90 bricks an hour, that in 1928 he took out a card as an adult apprentice in the Amalgamated Union of Building Trade Workers. The second lake was added in the 1930s and during its construction Churchill nearly lost a hired No. 4 Ruston Excavator which sank into the ooze. But on the lake's completion he could rest easy in the smug satisfaction that he now had an expanse of water larger than that at Churt, the estate of his some-time political ally and neighbour, David Lloyd George!

Claremont Landscape Garden, *SURREY* *
CLIVE OF INDIA

Clive of India had no love for the rather damp house he purchased in 1769, even if it was designed by the celebrated architect John Vanbrugh, its previous owner. He had it demolished and started building a new, much fancier edifice. Engaging 'Capability' Brown to oversee the house and gardens, Clive (another animal enthusiast) had him make a menagerie, which was home to African not, as one might expect, Indian fauna. The animals included 'a zebra and foal; 2 antelopes; 1 African bull; 28 Cape geese; 6 turkeys; 2 guinea fowl; 2 Chinese pencil'd pheasants; 2 pea fowl; and 5 curaso birds'.

Clive, or to give him his full title Robert, Baron Clive of Plassey, was an enigmatic and sadly troubled figure. And after spending so much money on his beloved house and garden, he never had the chance to live there. The son of a minor Shropshire squire, he had travelled to India in 1743 and entered the British East India Company's service a year later. After a period of depression, he eventually found his niche and proved himself an inspired administrator and superb military tactician, rising swiftly through the ranks. The 32-year-old's triumph at the Battle of Plassey in 1757 ended any French hope of remaining in India and laid the foundation for British dominance of the subcontinent that lasted until 1947. In reward he was appointed the first Governor of Bengal, but problems in his second stint as Governor (1765–6) led to jealous accusations of embezzlement against him. Despite parliamentary vindication in 1773, he was a broken man and committed suicide in 1774, never to enjoy the grand home that had been his life's work.

Hardwick Hall, *DERBYSHIRE* *
ELIZABETH TALBOT, COUNTESS OF SHREWSBURY
('BESS OF HARDWICK')

After Queen Elizabeth I (1533–1603), the second most powerful woman in the country at the time was Elizabeth Talbot, Countess of Shrewsbury (1527–1607), better known to posterity as Bess of Hardwick, a collector of husbands, who just loved having royalty to visit and built a house with that in mind. Though born into minor nobility, Bess, like her three sisters, was bequeathed the slight sum of £26 13s 4d when her father died in the year after her birth. But from these modest beginnings she built up a personal fortune through astute husbandry, working her way through four wealthy marriages and acquiring land and property. Her final marriage, to George Talbot, 6th Earl of Shrewsbury, began lovingly enough but ended in acrimony and Bess retreated to Hardwick which she had bought from her bankrupt brother in 1583 and which was undeniably hers. Here she began to rebuild the Old Hall. But when Shrewsbury died in 1590, she stopped work on that and began to build a completely new house a few hundred feet away.

Both buildings survive today in an extraordinary juxtaposition. With its great glittering windows and towers thrusting into the sky, the New Hall has been likened to a lantern. The state rooms where Bess would entertain her special guests were located at the top of the house to provide the best view down over the gardens below. Their arrangement can still be seen today, although the details of the knot beds have long vanished. However, it is possible to hazard a guess at what may have been planted: Bess like all educated Elizabethans loved allegories and allusions and one of the most popular was the cult of the Virgin Queen, giving her a chance to be suitably obsequious. Gardens were filled with plants that represented Elizabeth's perceived virtues, including lilies, foxgloves, irises (representing purity, stateliness and wisdom, respectively), and of course the rose, symbol of the Tudors. However, although we cannot be sure of how the gardens were actually planted, evidence of Bess's flattery still exists inside the house, where the plaster frieze that runs around the High Great Chamber is an allegorical celebration of the Virgin Queen. Elizabeth is represented by the chaste moon – goddess Diana, in the words of Ben Jonson, the 'Queen and huntress, chaste and fair'.

> *Elizabethans loved allegories and allusions and one of the most popular was the cult of the Virgin Queen ... Gardens were filled with plants that represented Elizabeth's perceived virtues*

Hughenden Manor, *BUCKINGHAMSHIRE* *
BENJAMIN DISRAELI

Home of Benjamin Disraeli (1804–81), Queen Victoria's favourite Prime Minister, Hughenden has colourful gardens designed by his wife, Mary Anne, and was a real 'labour of love' for both of them. Mary Anne developed an area of woodland to the north of their villa with rides cut through the plantations and called it a 'German forest'. Disraeli concentrated on the formal garden, writing proudly of it; 'we have made a garden of terraces, in which cavaliers might roam and saunter with their lady-loves'. Reputedly, Disraeli's response to a guest who complained about the noise of his resident wildlife was 'My dear lady, you cannot have a terrace without peacocks!'

Lyveden New Bield, *NORTHAMPTONSHIRE* *
SIR THOMAS TRESHAM

When he inherited the estate in 1559, Tresham (1543–1605) decided that he would love to have a terrace: a popular Elizabethan innovation influenced directly by the Italian style. No doubt, visiting friends, he had been impressed by similar features at Burghley House, Theobalds Park, Holdenby House and Kirby Hall. The ingenious aspect of the newly-fashionable terrace was that, being placed around the house, it united house and garden and the formal style was much in keeping with the current fashion for linear architectural design.

At Lyveden, the existing medieval manor house known as the Old Bield or Old Building stood in a modest enclosed garden, in an older style of the period. So Tresham extended the garden southwards towards the ridge of a valley where, on a newly-designed terrace, he erected a new garden lodge, the New Bield. Sir Thomas described his garden plans in his papers and, in conjunction with careful archaeological investigation, they reveal that somewhat concealed under the accumulation of 400 years of detritus the garden remains much the same as he intended it. It seems likely he planned to add a third storey to the New Bield, so that he and his guests might enjoy the wonderful view of his new 54-acre garden, set within 520 acres of deer park. In a letter to his staff, Tresham wrote 'if my moated orchard could in any part be prepared for receiving of some cherry trees and plum trees I like it well'. This implies that the central area was to be planted with an orchard of fruiting trees surrounded by canals, and further accounts make mention of four viewing mounds, two spiral and two pyramidal, one at each corner. Aerial photographs, taken by the Luftwaffe during World War II, reveal traces of a circular pattern with diagonal features, in keeping with the Elizabethan love of complex labyrinthine designs. Current opinion is that the centre of this area contained a maze pattern, surrounded with fruit trees and bordered by plantings of scented flowers and medicinal herbs. And it may be that Tresham's garden design also refers to the crypto-Catholic symbology this fervent believer used in the architecture of the New Bield, which remained unfinished. Its design made reference to the number three (representing the Holy Trinity) but also to five (the wounds of Christ) and seven (the Stations of the Cross and the instruments of the Passion). Such was the strength of Tresham's religion that he spent 15 years in prison and under house arrest, from where he had much time to plan his garden.

For more about Sir Thomas, see Rushton Hall, page 96.

Monk's House, EAST SUSSEX *
LEONARD & VIRGINIA WOOLF

A deep love of gardens and gardening has been an important ingredient in the creative processes of certain literati. Monk's House was a retreat for the troubled Virginia (1882–1941) and provided her with the setting for her short story 'In the Orchard'. On a more practical note, profits from *Mrs Dalloway* and *The Common Reader* (both dedicated to Virginia's lover and friend, Vita Sackville-West) paid for the installation of new water closets in the house! (See Sissinghurst Castle Garden on page 46 for more on Vita.) Working in the garden writing room, Virginia was able to surround herself with inspiring views and embark on three of her greatest novels, *To The Lighthouse*, *Orlando* and *The Waves*. She and Leonard entertained many of the Bloomsbury literary set here, enjoying leisurely games of bowls on the large open lawn. Tragically, Virginia, plagued by depression, drowned herself in the nearby river Ouse in 1941. Leonard (1880–1969) remained at Monk's House until his death.

> **Working in the garden writing room, Virginia was able to surround herself with inspiring views and embark on three of her greatest novels**

Montacute House, *SOMERSET* *
SIR EDWARD PHELIPS

Sir Edward Phelips (1560–1614) began to build the house we see today at Montacute in the 1590s. Often featured as a location for films, Montacute's impressive Elizabethan facade is somewhat reminiscent of Hardwick Hall. Ever pragmatic, and somewhat frugal, Queen Elizabeth I encouraged her noblemen to build grand houses and gardens which often, rather obsequiously, incorporated designs that praised and celebrated her reign. She 'rewarded' them by descending, court and all, for a summer or Progress visit at their expense. Some were happier to see her than others. But Elizabeth was so beloved (not to mention powerful) that her noblemen willingly obliged – even though she didn't always fulfil her side of the bargain and turn up!

One nobleman who made the effort in vain was Sir Edward Phelips. Edward, elected an MP in 1584, funded the building of Montacute from his successful law practice. Some considered Phelips 'over swift in judging', especially against Catholics: apparently he sentenced one man to death 'simply for entertaining a Jesuit'. He became Speaker (a supposedly neutral role) of the House of Commons in 1604, but was criticized for being too close to government particularly when, in 1606, he opened the prosecution's case against Guy Fawkes and the members of the Gunpowder Plot.

Phelips lavished funds on his estate and his ambitious garden plans are clear in a description of the 24 acres of new and formal gardens, first recorded in detail in 1667. The description, paraphrased below, showed that the gardens had evidently not changed much since their creation 70 years previously, though the approach to the building was changed in the 19th century, and the 'faire Court' is now the lawn in front of the house:

From the porch of the house, four steps descended into a large terrace walk paved with freestone – a high quality sand or limestone. This was furnished with rails and balustrades between high pillars and pyramids. From this terrace there were six steps down into a 'faire Court', with a freestone walk in the middle leading to a gatehouse. The court was enclosed by an ashlar (stone that has been cut into squares) wall topped with rails, balustrades, pyramids and 'turrets of ornament'. At each corner of the court were two turrets with lodging chambers and, in the middle, a gatehouse. Beyond was another large court, walled about, with several walks and rows of trees. On the north side was a bowling green surrounded by trees and a variety of 'pleasant walks, arbours and coppices, full of delight and pleasure'. To the north of the house was a walled garden, planted out with flowers and fruit. At the end of the east walk was a banqueting house 'arched with Freestone within and leaded on the toppe thereof' and, to the west, an orchard and a woodyard with 'necessary buildings' – the dairy, laundry, brewery, bakery, pigeon house. On the south side were more orchards and kitchen gardens with fish ponds 'all incompassed within a wall'. On the west side of the house there was a large court set with rows of elms and walnuts leading to the stables, barns and granary, with further fish ponds and a hop garden of about an acre and a half in dimension.

Osterley Park, *MIDDLESEX* *
ROBERT CHILD

Inheriting Osterley Park on his brother's death in 1763, Robert – a successful banker and MP – spent a great deal of time and money on developing his new estate. The main attraction at Osterley was probably its late 18th-century menagerie, containing many exotic birds, which could be observed in a rather romantic manner: reached by a rope-drawn ferry-boat, the menagerie was a walled park-within-a-park that, according to Agneta Yorke, describing it in 1772, was the 'prettiest place (I) ever saw … an absolute retreat, & fill'd with all sorts of curious and scarce Birds and Fowles, among the rest 2 numidian Cranes that follow like Dogs, and a pair of Chinese teale that have only been seen in England before upon the India paper'.

Polesden Lacy, *SURREY* *
THE HON. MR & MRS RONALD GREVILLE, EDWARD VII

The Hon. Ronald Greville (d.1908) bought the Polesden estate in 1906 and converted it into a house and garden fit for a King, in this case his great friend Edward VII, who visited regularly and was treated regally. The pet dog cemetery behind the house contains the grave of Edward VII's beloved Airedale, Caesar, and other treasured pets from the Greville family. The garden also contains the grave of Mrs Greville herself, a legendary and celebrated Edwardian hostess. It was not that unusual for someone to choose to be buried in their garden, the same final resting place going to Miss Rosalie Chichester at Arlington Court in Devon and to Thomas, 8th Lord Berwick, at Attingham Park in Shropshire.

The Hon. Mrs Margaret Greville's (1864–1942) money was inherited from her father, who had made a fortune in producing McEwan's Export Beer. It did not 'go off' in hot climates and so was enthusiastically lapped up by the grateful British Army. A great deal of the proceeds went into developing both the opulent interior of Polesden Lacy and its garden. It was a place that people loved to visit, both for the celebrated house parties and the elegant gardens, with their magnificent views across the North Downs.

Mr Smith, Mrs Greville's last Head Gardener reported being interviewed by her while in bed, instructing him to 'speak to me as if I were a man'. Under his control and using over 300 tons of coke a year, the garden's factory-scale greenhouses churned out '1000 carnations in 6-inch pots, 200 *Begonia* 'Gloire de Lorraine', 200 poinsettas and assorted other plants all destined to fill the house with colour. A complete row of frames alone were devoted to violets (*Viola* 'Prince of Wales'), which were Mrs Greville's favourite flower'. The busiest week for Polesden was Ascot, when about 20 guests would stay. In addition to the flowers for the house, the gardeners were expected to provide 'ten sprays of flowers to match the colour of the dresses and a similar number of [red or white] carnations for button holes'. Rather befitting Mrs Greville's ritzy style (the house had, after all, been remodelled by Mewes and Davis, the architects used by the Ritz hotel), when the property was left to the National Trust the endowment included a cellar stuffed full of the finest champagne.

Rushton Hall, *NORTHAMPTONSHIRE*
SIR THOMAS TRESHAM

Sir Thomas Tresham, who also owned Lyveden New Bield (see page 88–89) hid his papers in the walls of Rushton Hall after his son was implicated in the Gunpowder Plot. Rediscovered only recently, they offer an illuminating glimpse into his life and the gardens he created at his estates. At Rushton he designed and built the Triangular Lodge or 'warrener's lodge' as accommodation for the keeper of his rabbits. Tresham made a tidy sum supplying the London market with furs, so presumably wanted to keep him happy. Planned as an equilateral triangle, the lodge is also decorated with devices expressed in threes, to declare Tresham's devotion to the Trinity.

Married within his Catholic faith, to Muriel Throckmorton of Coughton Court in Warwickshire, both the Throckmortons and Sir Thomas remained true to their faith since they produced 12 children. In later years his religious devotion brought Sir Thomas perpetual persecution and from December 1581 onwards he was fined £20 a month for refusing to attend the Anglican Church. He was often imprisoned or placed under house arrest – which perhaps, at least, gave him time to think about designs for his garden. In the quarter century preceding his death, in 1605, he paid a total of just under £8,000 in penalties. His income (he received £2,000 per annum from rents and sheep alone) would have been sufficient to cover these costs had he not had larger expenditures. For, in addition to paying marriage portions for four of his six daughters and constantly bailing out his reckless and feckless son Francis, Sir Thomas had epicurean tastes: kitchen expenditure for the 10 months to Michaelmas 1588 was £456 15s 9d. In comparison, the cost of his building works over the 5½ years from 1591 was a modest £971 0s 11d. As it was, Thomas died a debtor, to the tune of £11,495 16s 1d. The story did not end happily: the workmen downed tools leaving Lyveden unfinished, his son Francis died prematurely and Thomas' widow spent the rest of her life servicing his debts.

Studley Royal Water Garden & Fountains Abbey, *NORTH YORKSHIRE* *
JOHN AISLABIE

As any enthusiastic gardener will no doubt appreciate, making a landscape can be a labour of love, and a form of therapy to sooth the soul. In 1720, when the South Sea Bubble burst, it was the Chancellor of the Exchequer, John Aislabie (1670–1742) – who had championed the South Sea Company's scheme to pay off the National Debt – who was held responsible for the stock market crash that brought ruination to thousands of speculators. In 1722, disgraced and with his political career over, the deeply embittered Aislabie (who blamed the Whig Prime Minister, Sir Robert Walpole, for masterminding his downfall) took refuge from the world at Studley Royal. For the next 20 years as a form of catharsis, Aislabie devoted himself to developing his eclectic garden, which more than tips its hat to the great formal French gardens of the 17th century at a time when fashion was moving towards the informal. Given his ambitious plans, he had clearly not lost *everything* in the stock market crash.

Set within stylized 'natural surroundings', Aislabie developed one of the finest formal water gardens in the country. The waters of the river Skell were tamed to create the long formal canal and large lake, the round pool and two crescent-shaped moon pools. Neat lawns were planted around the ponds and the canal was bounded by clipped yew hedges, turf embankments and ramps. Aislabie studded the woodlands with buildings, including a twisting grotto tunnel, an octagonal Gothic temple and a rotunda. Although the design was his, he seems to have been an awkward client when it came to the construction of his garden. Constantly interfering and frequently changing his mind, he drove John Simpson, his first works supervisor, to the point where he had to resign on the grounds of ill health. Simpson's replacement, Robert Doe, proved more adept at dealing with his picky patron – or perhaps was more able to 'turn a deaf ear'. A master mason from London, Doe was responsible for the various garden buildings and for the erection of the statuary.

To make things more complicated, the enthusiastic Aislabie wanted to include the neighbouring ruins of the mediaeval abbey of Fountains as part of his estate. In 1720 he had offered £4,000 for the ruins, but the deal fell through. In a fit of pique the delightful Aislabie raised an artificial hill on his land and capped it with a tent, enabling him to enjoy the view of the abbey, while simultaneously blocking his neighbour's view of Studley's attractive grounds.

Aislabie's son, William, finally managed to acquire Fountains Abbey estate for the princely sum of £16,000 in 1768 and proceeded to extend the garden below the lake, planting trees in the gorge, building a rustic zig-zag bridge across the river and setting eye-catching features on prominent outcrops. In the 1780s William Gilpin, popular writer on art, landscape and aesthetics, judged the acquisition of the Abbey ruins as a mixed blessing, complaining that as soon as William had got his hands on them 'he pared away all the bold roughness and freedom of the scene and given every part a trim polish'. No doubt this critical commentary had poor William turning in his grave because a Gilpin-inspired 'picturesque' effect was exactly what he had been trying so hard to achieve!

Tatton Park, *CHESHIRE* *
SIR JOSEPH PAXTON, LORD MAURICE EGERTON

Tatton Park has a long history of 'no expense spared' development by besotted owners. Already boasting a Humphry Repton landscape, Lewis Wyatt added the great orangery in 1818 and was succeeded by another famous greenhouse-maker, Joseph Paxton (1803–1865), knighted for his design for Crystal Palace, which housed the Great Exhibition of 1851. Paxton now brought his skills to Tatton, building the great balustraded parterre in 1856 and, three years later, adding a new fernery. The latter became home to New Zealand tree ferns, among which lurked a collection of pet snakes!

In a last flurry of construction in 1910, Allan de Tatton Egerton, 3rd Baron Egerton, imported a team of Japanese of garden designers and gardeners to make a Japanese garden, complete with its own Mt Fuji, a pool fed by four streams, stone lanterns, bridges, thatched tea-house and a Shinto temple. The garden's plantry was carried on by his son Maurice Egerton, 4th Baron Egerton (1874–1958), archly referred to by some as the 'bachelor baron'. A shy man, Maurice travelled extensively and was both a pioneering motorist and aviator, counting Orville Wright among his friends. As well as a love of rhododendrons which he planted extensively, he also had a lifelong interest in youth organisations and especially the Boys' Club at nearby Knutsford, which he founded and fostered. Maurice also allowed local lads to bathe in Tatton Mere, a fishing pool in the grounds. Newspapers of the time report (without comment, one assumes) how 'Some afternoons, Lord Egerton's white-sailed yacht would cruise across and "Lordy" as the boys nicknamed him, would shower them with peaches and other delicacies.'

wrath

'Extreme anger, aroused by real or imagined wrong-doing.'

Gardens are not often the site of great outpourings of wrath and usually garden owners are slow to anger, but when the pressure blows it is best to be well out of range. Often it was those who 'did' the gardening rather than those who enjoyed the fruits of other people's labours who became most wrathful. Perhaps this says something both about the way they were treated by their employers and also the level of control and power that they wielded within their own realm that allowed them to express such emotions with seeming impunity.

Clumber Park, NOTTINGHAMSHIRE *
KATHLEEN, 7TH DUCHESS OF NEWCASTLE-UNDER-LYNE, SAMUEL BRAKER

Clumber Park had a particularly dastardly Head Gardener, Samuel Braker, whose wrath was coupled with a rather dishonest tendency to falsify his tax returns, not to mention (sacrilege!) cheating at the Royal Horticultural Society Westminster Show. When his employer, Kathleen, 7th Duchess of Newcastle-Under-Lyne (1872–1955) harvested and shared 'his' prize bunch of grapes with her friends, without his permission, Braker wrote her a vitriolic letter expressing his fury.

He was probably one of the worst, but no landowner, however grand and titled, wanted to incur the wrath of their Head Gardener, whose position in matters horticultural was very powerful. In the 19th and early 20th centuries, a time of great horticultural improvements, technological developments and scientific advances, the Head Gardener had to keep abreast of all the latest changes and implement them in his domain. And that domain could be very large: not only the grand formal gardens adjacent to the house, but the wider pleasure grounds beyond, and – especially for a large country house – extensive produce gardens to provide fruit and vegetables for the estate. The Head Gardener bore a great deal of responsibility and had to ensure quality and excellence in the garden at all times. He might be expected to provide a most spectacular and extensive show of bedding plants on the terrace, an unusual new conifer from Japan thriving in the pinetum, a rare orchid looking at its peak in the conservatory, or out-of-season vegetables and fruits on the dinner menu. Perhaps it's not surprising that some Head Gardeners got more than a bit tetchy when their careful plans were disrupted or interfered with. And some Head Gardeners had their own agenda. Thomas King, Head Gardener at Devizes Castle, 'grew what flowers he preferred despite the family's wishes' and 'frustrated his employer's desire to have birds in the garden by breeding cats and cutting down roosting trees'.

The Head Gardener often commanded a large staff himself (until recent years, it was always 'he'), all of whom worked to keep the garden in tip-top condition. The story goes that when asked how many gardeners she employed Winnie, Duchess of Portland could not remember. She sent for her Head Gardener, who couldn't remember either and had to send for someone else. True or not, at the turn of the 20th century the gardening staff at large houses certainly could be huge: it was 100 at Waddesdon, 70 at Cragside, while the royal vegetable garden at Frogmore (which was only part of the Windsor Palace estate) employed one man for each of its 50 acres.

Hidcote Manor Garden, GLOUCESTERSHIRE *
LORD ABERCONWAY, GEORGE FORREST, LAWRENCE JOHNSTON, NORAH & NANCY LINDSAY

The National Trust was founded in 1895 to protect threatened countryside and buildings from the more uncontrolled ravages of industrialization. But it was not until 1947 that Henry McLaren Lord Aberconway (1879–1953), Chairman of the RHS and owner of Bodnant in Conwy, suggested that a joint committee be set up with the Trust, in order to protect a select number of Britain's finest gardens. A year later, Hidcote Manor became the first garden to be taken on under this scheme.

Lawrence Johnston (1871–1958) had intended to leave Hidcote to his great friend Norah Lindsay (1876–1948), who throughout the 1920s had given him expert advice on how to arrange his plants. A highly talented artist-gardener she could, according to her 1948 obituary in *The Times*, 'trace out a whole garden with the tip of her umbrella'. Norah's own garden at Sutton Courtenay in Oxfordshire was 'without grandeur, but not without formality', and she carefully cultured its (and her own) image in a 1931 *Country Life* article, observing 'some gardens, like some people, have a charm potent to enslave and yet as intangible as dew or vapour. The gardens of the manor of Sutton Courtenay have this shining quality.' Norah worked on the principle that 'wherever the flowers themselves have planned the garden, I gracefully retire, for they are the guiding intelligences and strike where we fumble', and her style was a romantic, abundant eclecticism that used rich masses of flowers including weeds and self-sown 'vagrants'. A social butterfly, Norah was a frequent guest of the Londonderry's at Mount Stewart; for the Astor's at Cliveden she converted the ribbon borders into herbaceous ones and for Lord Lothian at Blickling she replanted the overly-elaborate parterre that had been laid out in the 1870s.

Sadly Norah died before Johnston and the fact that he chose instead to leave Hidcote to the National Trust incurred the great wrath of her daughter, Nancy (d.1973), who had inherited neither her mother's graciousness nor her generosity. Upon discovering his plans she became somewhat viperous and obdurate. James Lees-Milne recounts that at the handing over of the property 'Miss Lindsay is like an old witch, very predatory and interfering. She maintains that she has been deputed by L.J. to supervise these gardens in his absence abroad. We were not overcome with gratitude.' Despite appointing herself the garden's unofficial 'guardian' during the National Trust's early years of management, Nancy is reputed to have burned all Johnston's gardening papers in a fit of anger. But the garden itself is testament to his skill. Hidcote is often compared to Vita Sackville-West's own garden at Sissinghurst. Both gardens command beautiful views, and both have as their main focus a varied series of inward-looking rooms that 'hang' from a carefully structured framework, filled with a jungle of diverse plants arranged as much for artistic effect as botanical interest. And although Sissinghurst's 'White Garden' now enjoys more fame, Hidcote boasted an earlier example of a monochrome display. The twin Red Borders (1914–20) are one of Hidcote's triumphs: the reds draw the eye to the foreground and bring the gazebos into sharp focus, which in turn provide a frame for the backdrop of the rich green Stilt Garden and, beyond, the hazy blue of the Gloucestershire sky.

An American born in Paris, Johnston became a naturalized British citizen and was certainly a brave man, fighting in both the Boer War and World War I, in which he was injured, buried alive and left for dead. Despite its hardships and dangers, soldiering must have given Johnston a welcome break from home. It's hard to believe that anyone could become angered in Hidcote's elegant surroundings, although Lawrence certainly had just cause to feel wrath towards his own mother, the twice widowed (and extremely wealthy) Gertrude Winthrop. Having purchased Hidcote in 1907, Mother lived there with Lawrence until her death in 1926 and kept a tight reign on both the financial purse-strings and her son. Lee-Milne described him in 1943 as 'a dull little man and just as I remember him when I was a child. Mother-ridden. Mrs. Winthrop, swathed in grey satin from neck to ankle, would never let him out of her sight.'

To add insult to injury, Gertrude left her fortune to more distant relatives and left her son only with the house and 'subsistence'. Perhaps she was punishing Johnston for his obstinate decision to become a gardener, rather than the farmer she would have preferred. But he pursued his chosen path with dedication, becoming a very knowledgeable plantsman, plant hunter and plant breeder. From China he re-introduced *Jasminum polyanthum*, which had been lost to cultivation, and also two new mahonias (M. *lomariifolia* and M. *siamensis*). He bred *Hypericum* 'Hidcote', but not, contrary to popular misconception *Geranium* 'Johnson's Blue'. A hybrid between G. *himalayense* and G. *pratense*, the latter was raised by Arthur Tysilio Johnson in about 1950.

In the wake of his mother's demise, Johnston decided to spread his wings and seek plants for his garden by visiting their native habitats. In 1927 he journeyed to South Africa as part of an expedition to Tanganyika, which included 'Cherry' Ingram (who made his garden at Rosemoor in north Devon) and Reginald Cory (whose garden was at Dyffryn, near Cardiff). But, somewhat unusually for a plant hunter, Johnston insisted on taking along his valet and chauffeur along for the ride. As Ingram tartly noted, these arrangements 'certainly added to his personal comfort, but seemed to me to be a bit of an extravaganza'. Two years later, aged 58, with only one lung and suffering from malaria, Johnston stumped up £500 and ventured to Yunnan in China to hunt for plants with George Forrest (1873–1932) on the great plant hunter's last journey.

Johnston's behaviour on what was to be an arduous expedition, certainly incurred the wrath of the determined and resourceful Forrest, an enigmatic chap who thoroughly enjoyed his life's work amid the stunning scenery of Western China. Patient and tactful when dealing with locals, the resilient and somewhat gruff Scot did not suffer fools gladly and Johnston angered and irritated him in the extreme. By September 1930 preparations were well under way for their first six-week trek which, Forrest complained, he had been left to equip, organize and pay for, while the selfish Johnston spent 'every day riding in the morning, tea and tennis in the afternoons and bridge at the club in the evening'. Johnston then became seriously ill, but insisted on continuing when he should have stayed in bed. In February 1931, when Forrest had 'escaped', leaving Johnston to recuperate in Bhamo while he proceeded on to Tengyueh on the Burmese/Chinese border. In a distinctly caustic letter to Professor William Wright-Smith, Forrest wrote both of his frustration with Johnston and his annoyance at himself for not listening to the warnings of others who advised not to take him along. Indeed, he was so fed up with the prevaricating Johnston that he exclaimed 'Had I raked GB with a small tooth comb couldn't have found a worse companion'! Noting that no-one in the field likes Johnston, Forrest gave full vent to his spleen, calling the hapless chap a 'right good old Spinster spoilt by being born male' adding that 'A person more utterly selfish I have yet to meet'. Beware the wrath of a thwarted plant hunter!

Melford Hall, *SUFFOLK* *
LADY HYDE-PARKER

The aristocratic fear of incurring your own Head Gardener's wrath was evidently so widespread that P G Wodehouse was able to include a familiar portrait of such an imperious and self-important character in his novel, *Lord Emsworth and the Girl Friend*, written in 1928. Given her own experience, Lady Hyde-Parker of would have found much to identify with in Wodehouse's fictional Head Gardener, McAllister, who has for years been trying to replace Lord Emsworth's beloved mossy walk with a gravel path. But when Lord Emsworth is about to have it out with his truculent employee he yet again realises 'how completely he was in this man's clutches.'

By earlier standards, Mr Pomfret the Head Gardener had a tiny workforce of only five under his command at Melford Hall, but his personality was certainly larger-than-life. With his attire – 'black bowler hat, a

Lady Hyde-Parker, of Melford Hall: 'If I took a peach from ... the garden on a summer's day, Pomfret knew at once ... he managed to convey that he knew perfectly well who the culprit was and that he disapproved strongly'

green baize apron covering the front of his black trousers and jacket, and a white shirt', and demeanour designed to ooze an aura of self-detached importance, Pomfret was master of all he surveyed in the gardens. And when Lady Hyde-Parker occasioned to take fruit from the kitchen garden without permission her employee he 'managed to convey that he knew perfectly well who the culprit was and that he disapproved strongly.'

sloth

'Reluctance to work or make
an effort; laziness.'

In many ways sloth is what a garden should be all about
– taking it easy, refreshing the mind and revivifying the
spirit. But gardeners never seem to achieve the appropriate
state of sloth. There is always some tinkering to do and
a level of insecurity that makes the gardener exclaim to
every summer visitor 'you should have seen it last week'
or 'you should come back next week, it'll be perfect then'.
But if there is a team of gardeners to do the worrying
as well as the weeding, a garden offers an almost
inexhaustible supply of opportunities for slothfulness.

Antony, *CORNWALL* *
RICHARD CAREW

Fishing was one recreation offered on the estate that forced those taking part to get in at least a little hard exercise after an afternoon of gluttony and hard drinking – and for some it became quite an obsession. The friendly, amusing, loyal, and highly educated Richard Carew (1555–1620) was a true Cornishman, publishing only the second county survey *The Survey of Cornwall* in 1602. He also penned a verse in celebration of his beloved fish-pond at Antony, which was created in around 1577:

'I wait not at the lawyer's gates,
Ne shoulder climbers down the stairs;
I vaunt not manhood by debates,
I envy not the miser's fears;
But mean [moderate] in state, and calm in sprite [spirit],
My fishful pond is my delight.'

Today, the current Sir Richard Carew-Pole has re-dug the 'fishful pond' (now filled with fresh rather than salt water) and plans to build the banqueting house that his namesake had commissioned from Sir Arthur Champernowne for the island, but never erected.

The bath house at Antony, built in 1788–90 by Reginald Pole-Carew (1753–1835), was more ornate and civilized than most, but not warm. Equipped with a panelled changing room, it had a peristyle courtyard surrounded by columns and a plunge bath filled with icy but no doubt beneficial salt water from the Tamar Estuary.

Baddesley Clinton, *WARWICKSHIRE* *
JOHN BROME

Fishing always offers ample scope for just hanging about doing nothing much. At Baddesley Clinton, John Brome (1432–69) dug three new fish ponds and stocked them at a cost of £4.16s.

Strange as it may seem, the tendency to have a pond full of edible, live fish originated in religious observance. The mediaeval church decreed that in order to mortify the flesh and reduce carnal passions, eating meat was forbidden on Fridays, during Lent and, until early Tudor times, on Saturdays and Wednesdays too. In total this accounted for about half the days of the year, so fish was on the menu quite a lot. A typical manor house would have its own fish pools, ideally a three pond system: one stocked with pike, another with less predatory fish and a third, the Stew, with those ready for the table or sale, divided to keep different types separate.

at Coughton Court ... 'ladies of the house were wont to fish leaning out of the windows'

In time, such pools often evolved into ornamental features filled with fish for sport. At Baddesley Clinton, John's earlier fish pond from 1444 became the Great Pool. A moat also made a handy place to raise or catch fish. Here, and at Coughton Court prior to Sir Robert Throckmorton draining it in 1780, 'ladies of the house were wont to fish leaning out of the windows'.

Basildon Park, BERKSHIRE *
JAMES MORRISON, WILLIAM TURNER

Basildon Park was the home of James Morrison (1789–1857), a wealthy haberdashery merchant, art collector, key player in the establishment of the National Gallery and Liberal MP. Morrison was a classic example of a Victorian merchant-prince. From humble beginnings working for London haberdashers, Todd & Co., he married the boss's daughter Mary Ann and, in 1814, took over the company. Turnover rose from £64,449 in 1813 to £650,570 in 1871 and, as well as devising the principle of 'small profits and quick returns', he also made a killing in 1821 when he cornered the market for black crêpe at the time of Queen Caroline's funeral (the wife of George IV).

But Morrison knew how to enjoy the fruits of his labours and in 1838 bought Basildon Park for £97,000.

> *William Turner ... was a particularly dedicated angler and regular guest at Basildon Park, replying to one invitation 'Mr Turner ... hopes he may bring his fishing tackle'*

Located a stone's throw from the River Thames, Basildon was the ideal place to get in a bit of lazy fishing and attracted some illustrious house guests who had this in mind. The great painter, William Turner (1775–1851), was a particularly dedicated angler and regular guest at Basildon Park, replying to one invitation 'Mr Turner begs to present his thanks for the kind invitation to Basildon in the course of this month or next and hopes he may bring his fishing tackle'.

Some 90 years later the house passed out of the family, sold by his nephew and heir, Major James Archibald Morrison. The Major, a 'proud and corpulent' man, had insisted on walking rather than crawling when under enemy fire during World War I. He inherited a second fortune from his father, but still managed to fritter both away on an extravagant lifestyle, three marriages and a passion for country pursuits. Legend has it the directors of the paper company Millington & Sons, while enjoying a shooting party at Basildon in 1911, came up with the name 'Basildon Bond' for their new brand of writing paper.

Chartwell, *KENT* *
SIR WINSTON CHURCHILL

A lesser-known fact about Winnie is that during World War II, whenever he could snatch time, he would hurry from London to Kent to visit the golden orfe fish that lived in his lake, which he adored. This passion continued after the war when, according to Victor Vincent, who gardened at Chartwell from 1947, Churchill looked forward to receiving the weekly tin of maggots with which he delighted in feeding his beloved pet fish. We don't know Churchill's response to Stalin who, during a conference in World War II, was told of Winston's fondness for his goldfish and tactlessly asked 'would you like some for breakfast?'

Churchill was also partial to swimming but, sensibly, not in cold water. The 1930s obsession with the health-giving benefits of outdoor recreation had resulted in a rash of unheated public lidos and private pools, but at Chartwell coke-fired boilers kept Winston's pool balmy and if he thought that the water was getting too cold, he was known to get out and stoke the boilers himself.

Chastleton House, *OXFORDSHIRE* *
WALTER WHITMORE-JONES

With the exception of Robert Catesby, leader of the Gunpowder Plot, Chastleton has not been home to many 'celebrity' owners. But Walter Whitmore-Jones (1831–72), who lived there in the 1800s, can lay a small claim to fame. In the 1860s he converted the bowling green into a croquet lawn and set about developing all kinds of variations on what some regard as the most vicious and vindictive of all sports. Though croquet in some form can be dated back to the 1600s, Whitmore-Jones was the first to codify clear rules. In 1865 these were published by *The Field* and when the first championship was held three years later at Evesham in Worcestershire, the unsporting Walter entered and, naturally, won. Croquet quickly became popular, especially with women, who relished the chance to 'play' outside in mixed company, albeit with chaperones. Visitors can still play croquet on his hallowed turf. No doubt Walter would be pleased to know that occasionally games are still played, but he must have turned in his grave at Churchill's unorthodox approach to the game. A good polo player in his youth, Winnie apparently brandished the mallet single-handed, a definite *faux pas*.

Walter seems to have been an imaginative egotist with strong powers of persuasion. Griping that his superiors were fools, he left his job as a clerk in the Audit Office (a post offered to him by Disraeli himself) in favour of a life composing doggerel verse, inventing silly gadgets (for example, a bootlace-winder ideal for the lazy gent), and developing board games. He was quite successful at the latter and had several accepted by the famous firm of John Jaques in the 1860s, including Squails, The Imperial Chinese Game of Frogs and Toads, and The Game of War. It appears that, for some people, a life of sloth and leisure definitely has its rewards.

Claremont Landscape Garden, *SURREY* *
QUEEN VICTORIA, SIR JOHN VANBRUGH

Just as gentlemen did not work, so owners did not make gardens themselves – they 'had them made' by others and simply enjoyed the results. Behind tall walls and locked gates, these private sanctuaries offered many opportunities for relaxation. Faced with a difficult life of non-employment and inherited wealth, there was nothing to do but find various pleasurable activities to while away all those non-working hours. Paintings and photographs show that, pernicious weather permitting, picnics, afternoon tea, musical recitals, readings, or simply just relaxing and entertaining friends outdoors were all pastimes enjoyed by the leisured class.

Queen Victoria (1819–1901) had fond memories of pleasant, lazy times at Claremont, writing that it was 'the brightest epoch of my otherwise melancholy childhood'. Returning in later life with her husband, the couple enjoyed taking a lazy breakfast outside under a large oak on the Mount. Perhaps inspired by the Queen, who as a widow preferred to conduct much of her business from a tent set up in the gardens at Osborne House, on the Isle of Wight, *al fresco* living became popular.

Claremont boasts a bowling green, which overlooks the Belvedere and is a charming building itself, built to a design by Sir John Vanbrugh, equipped with a bar and tables for playing dice. For the more energetic, a nine-pin alley (or skittles) was situated behind a small Tuscan temple, sadly now demolished. The bowling green was essentially an evolutionary step in the development of that icon of the English garden, the immaculately manicured lawn, which in many forms became a smooth, verdant surface for all sorts of leisurely diversions. To successfully roll a bowl required perfect sward. Thus it was essential the green be only grass and kept free of weeds. To achieve the necessary closely shorn finish in the years before Mr Budding developed his cylinder mower in the 1830s (even then it took a while to catch on), the lawn was trimmed by skilful scythe men, who adjusted the height of the cut by adjusting the height of their shoe soles.

Bowls may have been invented by the Egyptians and a game called *bocce* was certainly popular with Rome's legions. If they did not bring it to these shores, then the Normans certainly did: the Old Bowling Green Club established in Southampton in 1299 still remains active. But if Sir Francis Drake had been playing on Plymouth Hoe in July 1588 rather than waiting for the tide to turn, he would have been breaking the law. For in 1541 Henry VIII had banned playing bowls in public in a failed attempt to keep young men at the archery butts. The flip side of Henry's Act, which was finally repealed in 1845, was to grant private bowls licences to landowners. Thus a green in your garden became desirable, not just because it provided a diversion, but also because to have a green was to have a licence and to have a licence was to 'be someone'.

Greens were made across the country and down the centuries – one was included as part of the 17th-century garden at Chastleton, while Bridgeman made the one at Claremont in around 1725.

Queen Victoria, on Claremont: 'the brightest epoch of my otherwise melancholy childhood'

Cliveden, *BUCKINGHAMSHIRE* *
GEORGE HAMILTON, EARL OF ORKNEY, FREDERICK, PRINCE OF WALES

As the habit of banqueting in the garden died out in the 1700s, so taking tea became all the rage instead. At Cliveden the Venetian architect Giacomo Leoni designed an Octagon temple (c.1735), where Lord Orkney (1666–1737) enjoyed both his tea and the spectacular views down over the River Thames below.

Cliveden was also the scene of a fatal sports injury. Frederick, Prince of Wales, may have died in 1751 as a result of a blow received from a cricket ball while playing a match in the grounds. But you can never trust a cricketing 'tall tale': another version has it that gardening killed him, when he caught a fatal chill as a result of getting soaked while directing works in his garden at Kew in Surrey.

Croome Park, *WORCESTERSHIRE* *
GEORGE WILLIAM, 9TH EARL OF COVENTRY

A leisurely dip in the pool is one thing, but George William, 9th Earl of Coventry (1838–1930), took things a little too far. Finding a natural saline spring that bubbled up in the village of Defford, situated on his estate, he heated the water and filled two relaxing spa baths – one for him, and the other for his horses.

Dudmaston, *SHROPSHIRE* *

Today we tend to think of relaxing in the pool as the epitome of laziness, but poolside living in the 1700s was a little more spartan. Even so, the outdoor Ladies' Bath created at Dudmaston sounds delightful, if a tad chilly, consisting of a series of three small oval, interconnected and tiered pools fed by a natural spring.

Generally, bathing in the 18th century had been undertaken for reasons of health rather than hygiene. Mineral spring water was considered an elixir and visiting a spa town to 'take the waters' was part of the social scene. The 1707 treatise *Practical Dissertation on the Bath Waters* by Dr Oliver advocated immersion in cold water to cure a host of ailments ranging from impotence to headaches. For many years William Oliver was one of the leading physicians in the spa town of Bath and gained fame and fortune as the inventor of the Bath Oliver biscuit. And since many people who visited spa towns wished to continue their 'treatment' at home, baths either inside, or outside in the form of a garden bath house, became increasingly popular.

Hardwick Hall, *DERBYSHIRE* *
ELIZABETH TALBOT, COUNTESS OF SHREWSBURY
('BESS OF HARDWICK')

The concept of banqueting in the garden, in particular eating sweetmeats – the final course of a meal – had became fashionable in Tudor times. Bess of Hardwick had no fewer than four banqueting houses: two in the garden, one in a loggia and one on the leads of the roof of the New Hall from which she and her more intrepid guests could enjoy dining in a leisurely fashion, in much more intimate surroundings than the large state rooms that were used for formal dining. Their menu was likely to include spiced wine and sweetmeats or marmalade sorbets. The latter, made from the still-exotic and rare orange and ice, required careful storage and amply demonstrated the host's wealth and sophistication – not to mention horticultural prowess.

Knightshayes Court, *DEVON* *
LADY AMORY

During World War II, United States Air Force personnel convalescing at Knightshayes Court were kept distracted by the fiendishly difficult putting green. This was the plaything of Lady Amory, who in the 1920s and 1930s had been known as the 'Queen of the Links'. As Joyce Wethered (1901–97) she had dominated lady's golf, winning the English Ladies' Championship four times, the British Ladies' Open five times and the Worplesdon Mixed Foursomes eight times. Golf as we know it originated on the east coast of Scotland in the 15th century and the earliest reference is James II of Scotland's 1457 decree banning golf and football for the same reason that Henry VIII later proscribed bowls – as being too distracting for the young men who should be perfecting their archery skills instead. Charles I popularised golf in England, indeed it's said that he was playing a round when he was informed of the 1641 Irish Rebellion. The first international match was in 1682 when Scotland beat England and the first rules of golf were laid down in 1744.

Knole Park, *KENT* *
LORD JOHN SACKVILLE & JOHN FREDERICK SACKVILLE

The Sackvilles of Knole were especially cricket-obsessed. Lord John Philip Sackville (1713–65), brother of the 2nd Duke of Dorset, actually organized the first match for which a score card survives (England v. Kent, on 18 June 1774). Sadly though, John suffered from depression and was shabbily treated by his heartless relatives, who exiled him to Switzerland to subsist on a tiny allowance. The 3rd Duke, John Frederick (1745–99), known affectionately as 'the gay Duke' was just 24 when he inherited Knole and he devoted all his energies and wealth to 'Knole, love affairs and cricket'. His mistress, the famous ballerina and the subject of Gainsborough's eponymous-titled painting, Giovanna Baccelli (she was also painted by Reynolds), even gave John Frederick a gift of cricket bat and stumps.

> *The Sackvilles of Knole were especially cricket-obsessed. Lord John Sackville … organized the first match for which a score card survives*

John not only played cricket, but also employed a small squad of professional cricketers. One of the team was the bowler 'Lumpy' Stevens, who in a 1775 match between Kent and Hambledon in Hampshire, bowled several balls through his opponent's wicket (at a time when only two stumps were used, leaving a big gap). His accuracy led in part to the introduction of the third stump, used for the first time two years later when England played Hambledon at Sevenoaks. The Hambledon club, formed in the 1760s, established the batting and bowling process still used today, and claims to be the birthplace of cricket.

The real origins of cricket are lost in the mists of time, although the household accounts of Edward I for the year 1300 mention a cricket-like game played between Prince Edward and his friend Piers Gaveston in Kent. Indeed it's possible that the game originated on the sheep-grazed meadows of the south-east, possibly played by shepherds. The first recorded match took place at Coxheath in Kent in 1646, but cricket remained an essentially rural pastime until it became 'gentrified' in the 18th century and the first match between counties was at Dartford, when Surrey played Kent on 29 June 1709, though at that time there were still no established rules. Cricket continued to be very fashionable amongst the upper crust, who probably enjoyed its lazy pace and the chance to spend an afternoon lolling around in the English countryside.

Melford Hall, *SUFFOLK* *
QUEEN ELIZABETH I

England's fickle climate has always made garden buildings a popular and frequent refuge and their form is as diverse as the entertainments they hosted. Banqueting houses were often placed on top of mounts to provide an enjoyable view over the garden below but, sadly, most mounts and their buildings have long since vanished. One that has survived can be found at Melford Hall, where Queen Elizabeth I was entertained in 1578 and served by '200 young gentlemen cladde all in white velvet and 300 of the graver sort apparelled in black ... with 1500 servying men all on horseback'. Built by Sir William Cordell, the Octagon Pavilion is a useful combination of both look-out tower and banqueting house perhaps ideal for those who were just too lazy to get up from dessert when the enemy arrived, or for those who wished to indolently take a pot-shot at any passing game foolish enough to stray within bow shot.

Osterley Park, *MIDDLESEX* *
1ST EARL OF BALFOUR

On one famous Sunday in 1895, a private secretary to the Tory leader
Lord Salisbury arrived at Osterley Park hot, out of breath, and gasping
the words 'Give me an egg beaten up in brandy and find me Arthur
Balfour'. Balfour (1848–1930), who was playing tennis on the lawn at
the time, was then informed that the Liberal government had fallen
and he was back in power. With Drake-like coolness, Balfour first
finished his match before returning to London to take up position as
leader of the Conservatives.

Whatever the truth of this anecdote, tennis or, rather, lawn tennis
(another 19th-century invention) has always been a popular pursuit
among the leisured classes. Tennis itself can be traced back to the
French *jeu de paume* or
'game of the palm', a
game that was played
with a glove and
originated in France in
the 12th century. The
racket appeared in the
16th century and,
together with a leather
ball stuffed with wool
or hair, Real or Royal

*Lawn tennis was invented
in 1873 by Major Walter
C Wingfield, who
christened it the none-
too-catchy sphairistiké
('ball playing' in Greek)*

tennis became a royal favourite. Both the courts at Petworth (rebuilt
in 1845) and Henry VIII's original one at Hampton Court Palace in
Middlesex are still played. When Charles Goodyear perfected the
vulcanization process, patented in 1843, he enabled the fabrication of
a bouncy rubber ball (and a lot else, besides). Lawn tennis was invented
in 1873 by Major Walter C Wingfield, who christened it the none-too-
catchy *sphairistiké* ('ball playing' in Greek). With an hourglass-shaped
court, the first match was played at a garden party at Nantclywd in

Wales and the following year Wingfield received a patent for the game which was quite impossible to enforce. The All England Croquet Club at Wimbledon helped to establish the rules of lawn tennis and a new rectangular court shape, and hosted the first (male only) World Championship in 1877; the first women's competition was played seven years later. Lawn tennis quickly became very popular and of course remains so today, though not just for the gentry!

Sheffield Park Garden, *WEST SUSSEX* *
HENRY HOLROYD, 3RD EARL OF SHEFFIELD

In 1876 Henry Holroyd, 3rd Earl of Sheffield (1832–1909) inherited Sheffield Park. A career diplomat, the Earl was also a fanatical amateur cricketer. Though some might say the only thing slower than watching cricket is playing it, the Earl was obviously no slouch. Good enough to play for the Gentlemen of Sussex, one of his first priorities when moving in to Sheffield Park was to lay a new cricket pitch and, as president of the club, he was to spend thousands of pounds providing coaching for young players.

Between 1884 and 1896 the visiting Australian team opened their tour with a match against Lord Sheffield's XI. At the final match, attended by the Prince of Wales and over 25,000 freely admitted spectators, Sheffield's team included W G Grace as Captain (he made 49 in the first innings). In January 1891 a cricket match was played on the frozen third lake, but the following winter and in ailing health, which prevented him playing cricket himself, Sheffield instead financed Grace's team to tour Australia, where, to promote an inter-state competition, the Earl sponsored the Sheffield Shield. This is still competed for today, now under the name 'Pura' Cup.

Stowe Landscape Gardens, *BUCKINGHAMSHIRE* *
LORD AND LADY COBHAM

At Stowe, Lord Cobham and his male pals could retire to the Temple of Friendship to drink copious quantities of port from the cellars below and to discuss politics. Not to be outdone, Lady Cobham and her companions could withdraw to the Ladies' Temple (now known as the Queen's Temple) to gossip, take tea and do needlework.

But, after all this imbibing, it was a long way back to the house if you got caught short. At Stowe, as at many other houses, there was a very welcome and practical Necessary House. The building of 'ye Necessary house in ye Gardain' is mentioned in the 18th-century accounts for Belton House in Lincolnshire and the precise instructions given by William Windham II to his agent Robert Frary for the new one at Felbrigg Hall leave no doubt over its intended use:

'Should not the inside be stuccoed, or how do you do it? How many holes? There must be one for a child; and I would have it as light as possible. There must be a good broad place to set a candle on and a place to keep paper. I think the holes should be wide and rather oblong, the seats broad and not quite level, and rather low before, but rising behind. Tho' the better the plainer, it should be neat.'

zeal

'Great energy or enthusiasm for a cause or objective.'

Making a garden may be a source of pride, particularly for those who regard such a creation as a status symbol. But, as with every activity, gardening has its band of dedicated devotees who do it for the enjoyment and pleasure it affords. For many members of this sect, plants have become a passion – and in some cases an all-consuming obsession. Plantaholics have spent fortunes and gone to great lengths to grow the newest and the rarest blooms and to develop great collections. To these devotees we owe a great deal, for it is they who pushed forward the boundaries of the art and science of horticulture – as well as teaching the occasional salutary lesson.

Benthall Hall, *SHROPSHIRE* *
GEORGE MAW

Victorians were zealous plant collectors, and among their particular favourites were the alpine plants. Not only were alpines suitably exotic and different, but they were satisfyingly fiddly to grow successfully, offering another opportunity to demonstrate horticultural skills. Alpines were either grown in a rockery, a habitat created to suit the needs of alpines, or in a garden feature made of rocks. One of the 19th century's great alpinists was George Maw of Benthall Hall (1832–1912). His garden was of modest scale, but he went to great lengths to get his plants. His passion for alpines and bulbous plants gave him an escape from his 'day job' as a manufacturer of ornamental tiles. Deciding that the best way to secure new plants was to 'go native' and collect from the wilds, Maw undertook 25 plant hunting trips between 1869 and 1878, to numerous parts of Europe, the United States and Canada. In 1871 he accompanied Sir Joseph Hooker on the great botanist's penultimate plant-hunting trip to the Atlas Mountains in North Africa. Among Maw's discoveries were (referred to by their old names) *Chionodoxa luciliae* which bloomed for the first time at Benthall in 1877, *Saxifraga mawiana*, *Boerhavia maroooana*, *Draba mawi*, *Stachys mawiana*, *Ononis mawiana*, and *Crocus corsicus*. Maw was particularly fond of the last of these, publishing the now-rare *Monograph of the Genus Crocus* in 1886.

> ***Victorians were zealous plant collectors, and among their particular favourites were the alpine plants ... they were satisfyingly fiddly to grow***

Biddulph Grange Garden, STAFFORDSHIRE *
JAMES AND MARIA BATEMAN

If ever there was a marriage of 19th-century plant obsessives, it was that of Mr and Mrs Bateman. In 1840, after two years of marriage, James (1811–97) and Maria set up home at Biddulph Grange, extending the existing vicarage in the Italianate style and adding a terrace and a series of conservatories to house their collections of camellias, ferns, rhododendrons and orchids. From the outset the windy and exposed site dictated that, in contrast with the outward looking formal terraces and carefully choreographed pleasure grounds of other contemporary creations, a sheltering perimeter pinetum and arboretum was necessary for protection, so the Batemans created a fairytale inward-looking garden, with a labyrinthine sequence of ingeniously linked garden compartments.

The parterre on the terrace, with its stone dressing enclosed by yew hedges, featured roses, verbenas, and monkey puzzle trees (*Araucaria araucana*, introduced *en masse* by William Lobb from Chile in 1844), while the Dahlia Walk was laid out with yew buttresses, dividing the blocks of colours. The Italian Garden also took advantage of the sloping ground and led down to the Rhododendron Ground, the latter containing the first of the dramatic rockworks that are such a feature of Biddulph, designed by the marine artist Edward Cooke (1811–80).

Bateman first met Cooke in 1847 and he came to take a significant role in the garden's design, arranging massive pieces of local grit stone to look like naturally formed outcrops, planted with bilberries and heathers gathered from Biddulph moor. This natural backdrop was then exoticized by the addition of rhododendrons and azaleas, some of which had been collected by plant hunters sponsored by James. Other garden features incorporated by the enthusiastic Batemans included a rocky Glen, planted with rhododendrons and ferns that flourished in the moist, shady microclimate and a Chinese garden. Here the Batemans brought a willow pattern plate to life, building a wooden bridge over a pool and erecting a Chinese bridge, pagoda and temple designed by Cooke. There was a dragon parterre attended by a gilded water buffalo, a stone frog and even rockwork to imitate the Great Wall, complete with a look-out tower.

the pinetum and the arboretum were very much in keeping with Victorian enthusiasms ... both pleased the artist's eye and satisfied the contemporary enthusiasm for offering 'instruction'

And the whole was filled with newly introduced shrubs and trees from the Far East, particularly those discovered by plant hunter, Robert Fortune (1812–80) *Acer palmatum* 'Rubrum', *Abelia chinensis*, *Viburnum plicatum* 'Sterile', *Forsythia viridissima*, *Weigela florida*, *Jasminum nudiflorum*, *Lonicera fragrantissima* and three mahonias (M. *japonica*, M. *japonica* 'Bealei' and M. *fortunei*). Among other features were a Cheshire Cottage, built as a compliment to Maria's home county, with the initials 'J and M B' and the date of construction, 1856, emblazoned on the wall. This cosiness was offset by an Egyptian pyramid that, most disconcertingly, was accessed via the cottage. Inside, the rotund, rather grotesque figure of the ape of Thoth (an Egyptian deity associated with writing, wisdom and the moon) was, and is, eerily bathed in the light coming through a red glass skylight. Outside the temple, two pairs of sphinxes guard the way, implacably set against a background of yews, clipped into the shape of obelisks.

Despite such strange juxtapositions, James Bateman was particularly concerned with how nature and art could contrast harmoniously within a garden and the contrasting features and plantings reflect this enthusiasm. There has been much debate about the inspiration for the Batemans' 'world image garden'. In the 1840s, educated men were still concerned about the accurate and impending date of the last judgement and another possible inspiration suggested by garden historian Brent Elliott, in his book *Victorian Gardens* (1986), was that 'as a preliminary to the second coming, the world was once again bringing all its past history into light; and the garden at Biddulph Grange, by evoking vanished and alien civilizations, served as an affirmation that the millennium was coming'. Another school of thought has suggested it was inspired by the Great Exhibition of 1851, with its exhibits from countries all around the world.

But how did James and Maria come to have such zeal for gardens and exotic plants? James had been brought up at nearby Knypersley Hall, scion of a family made rich from engineering and interested in horticultural pursuits. So, inevitably, he had a zealous passion for plants from an early age, in particular orchids with which he became fascinated from the age of eight. As an Oxford undergraduate he visited the local nursery of Mr Fairbairn (who had once worked for the famous naturalist, Sir Joseph Banks), and it was here that he acquired a specimen of the orchid *Renanthera coccinea*, which had first flowered at Chatsworth, Derbyshire in 1827. Bateman was now irrevocably addicted to orchids and in 1833, while still a student at Magdalen College, he and his father privately funded Fairburn's foreman, Thomas Colly, to search British Guiana for new species of orchids. Colly came up with some 60 species, but Bateman was able to locate even more through his meeting with George Ure Skinner in 1834. Skinner, a Leeds merchant and amateur botanist, had a trading company in Guatemala and was persuaded to send orchids to Bateman. Many were new to science and Skinner's consignments provided most of the material for Bateman's book, *Orchidaceae of Mexico and Guatemala*, which he published at the tender age of 26. Only 125 copies of what he called the 'librarian's nightmare' (it remains the largest botanical book ever produced) were printed, but the tome established Bateman's international botanical reputation. However, he did not forget Skinner, who is remembered in the orchid Bateman requested his new friend, the horticulturist Dr Lindley, name for him *Barkeria skinneri*.

Maria's zeal for plants also started in her youth. She was born Maria Sibylla Egerton-Warburton, into a Cheshire family of equally enthusiastic gardeners who gardened at Arley Hall (where one of the first modern herbaceous borders was made in the 1840s). Maria also developed a passion for herbaceous plants, but her real enthusiasm was lilies: she became so knowledgeable about them that she earned herself the sobriquet 'that distinguished liliophile'.

The Batemans also planted trees enthusiastically and, today, their pinetum is noted for its huge specimens of monkey puzzle and other exotic conifers introduced from the Americas, Indo-China and Japan. Prior to David Douglas' exploration of the Pacific north-west of America in the mid-1820s and early 1830s, the arboretum – a collection of broad-leaved, deciduous and largely native trees – was also popular. Both the pinetum and the arboretum were very much in keeping with Victorian enthusiasms: taxonomical and geographical collections, in particular, both pleased the artist's eye and satisfied the contemporary enthusiasm for offering 'instruction' to the visitor.

While the less zealous planted rhododendrons in beds and shrubberies or used them to augment existing planting displays, purists insisted on having a collection. And, naturally, the Batemans planted a collection. In the second half of the 19th century Victorian gardens experienced the obsession of 'rhododendromania'. This was kick-started by the plant hunter Sir Joseph Hooker (1817–1911), during his four-year (1847–51) exploration of the then-Kingdom of Sikkim in the eastern Himalayas. A close friend and confidant of Charles Darwin, Hooker in later life succeeded his father as the second Director of Kew in 1865. Hooker's newly-discovered rhododendrons were extra-ordinary, but more used to the extreme temperatures of a

James Shirley Hibberd (in 1871): 'The money spent on rhododendrons during twenty years in this country would nearly suffice to pay off the National Debt'

Himalayan winter: they weren't going to survive in the wet cold that characterizes the British version. To get round this obstacle, horticulturists crossed his new species with their European and North American cousins, to create the 'Hardy Hybrids'. These exotic, brightly coloured and evergreen plants appealed hugely to the Victorian taste for novelty and a display of art in the garden, and planting rhododendrons in the pleasure grounds became an obsession for many wealthy gardeners. Writing in 1871, James Shirley Hibberd, later founder and first editor of *Amateur Gardening* magazine, noted that 'The money spent on rhododendrons during twenty years in this country would nearly suffice to pay off the National Debt' – a figure that stood at some £796 million at the time.

After many years of spectacular and frantic horticultural activity, the Batemans sadly found that the upkeep of the garden was beyond even their generous means. Passing Biddulph on to their son in 1884, they retired to Home House, near Worthing in West Sussex. Although they were by now in their seventies, they proceeded to transform this pocket handkerchief garden into what the *Gardeners' Chronicle* referred to as 'a little paradise'. Here they constructed a miniature mountain range to enable them to grow some of the plants that had not flourished at Biddulph, such as Hooker's Sikkim rhododendrons and Moutan peonies, along with *Lilium batemanniae*, a Japanese interspecific hybrid named after Maria in 1879. It seems likely that they grew the two clematis types that are now household names, 'Mrs James Bateman' and 'Miss Bateman'.

Bodnant Court, *NORTH WALES* *
HENRY MCLAREN, 2ND LORD ABERCONWAY

Harold Comber, the plant hunter son of the Head Gardener at Nymans, was partly funded on his expeditions by Henry McLaren, 2nd Lord Aberconway, whose garden was noted for its botanical collections. Henry also subscribed to many of the other financial consortia that sponsored similar expeditions by Frank Kingdon-Ward, Joseph Rock, Frank Ludlow, George Sherrif and George Forrest (see Hidcote Manor, page 102). Forrest was most famous for the discovery and introduction of over 300 new species of *Rhododendron* and, when he died in 1932, his Lordship continued to pay his native collectors to find and send seed for a further seven years. It was these arrivals that formed the basis of the 'McL' introductions, which Aberconway carefully nurtured at Bodnant where, incidentally, in the canal on the Rose Garden terrace, Sir Bernard Fryberg practised for his unsuccessful cross-Channel swim!

Like many, Aberconway was both a zealous grower and exhibitor of rhododendrons (see Biddulph Grange, page 125), and became fiercely competitive with another fancier Lionel de Rothschild of Exbury Gardens in Hampshire. At 'show time' Henry would commission a special train to transport his prized specimens from North Wales to the RHS Halls in London. Here, once his cherished specimens were exhibited to his Lordship's exacting standard, a butler in full dress would serve lunch from a hamper. However, both Aberconway and Rothschild were also very generous. For three years, from 1948, Aberconway sent a lorry-load of Bodnant plants to nearby Plas Newydd as a wedding present for Lord and Lady Anglesey in the care of two gardeners 'equipped', as its owner Lord Anglesey recalls, 'with shiningly polished spades to plant them'. Many of these were the famous Bodnant *Rhododendron* hybrids from *R. griersonianum*.

Cragside House, NORTHUMBERLAND *
GEORGE, 1ST LORD ARMSTRONG

In the 19th century the famous plant hunters Sir Joseph Hooker and Robert Fortune also published best selling accounts of their travels. Their vivid tales of adventures amid rugged and dramatic wild landscapes influenced new changes in garden-making fashion. As nature was 're-rediscovered', formal gardens lost their allure, and there was a new fad for creating imitation natural scenes. The most popular theme was that of the dramatic rhododendron forest, in imitation of the Himalayan valleys described in Hooker's *Himalayan Journals* (1854). The most spectacular imitation was made at the aptly-named Cragside, the creation of Lord Armstrong.

Lord Armstrong (on creating the gardens at Cragside): 'I could not give the faintest idea of the pleasure it has afforded me ... it has been my very life'

Born in Newcastle-upon-Tyne, William George Armstrong was one of that particularly Victorian breed of polymath who 'made it' by dint of hard work, self-determination, an intellectual and innovative mind, and a slice of timely good luck. Yet through his long and busy life he remained a very well-balanced man, variously described by contemporaries as 'loyal', 'considerate', 'kind', 'assured', 'generous', 'a wise delegator' and 'a good judge of character'. A delicate child, Armstrong came from a wealthy family and enjoyed an agreeable childhood. His 'earliest recollections consist of paddling in the river Coquet, gathering pebbles on its gravel beds, and climbing amongst the rocks on the Crag', where his house was to be built some five decades later. Although he trained as a lawyer, his passion was always amateur science – in particular hydraulics and electricity (see Cragside, page 32). One of his most financially rewarding inventions was the development of hydraulically powered quayside cranes in Newcastle in 1846. Following this success, W G Armstrong & Company was established in 1847 and one of its great claims to fame was the provision of the lifting gear for London's Tower Bridge. Opened in 1894, the original equipment is still in use today. Armstrong's next big innovation came in the aftermath of the Crimean War (1853–6). One of most serious criticisms levelled against the army was the pitiable state of its ordnance, which had changed little since the Battle of Waterloo in 1815. Armstrong was determined to develop a new heavy gun with breech-loading (for speed of reloading) and a rifled barrel (for accuracy). To this end he established the Elswick Ordnance Company, which made him his fortune.

By the early 1870s Armstrong had become more of a company figurehead than active director and had the leisure to turn his talents and fortune towards generous philanthropy and to developing Cragside, which he had purchased in 1863. Today conservationists would balk at his behaviour, but in the 18th century nobody blinked an eyelid at Armstrong's 'improvements', as he excavated and blasted away in order to dramatize the already impressive natural landscape and to create a level setting for his house. From 1869–84, architect R Norman Shaw remodelled and enlarged the existing house – by the time he had finished, it would also claim to be the first in the world to be lit by hydroelectricity.

With more than enough zeal to go around, Armstrong spent 'the whole of his spare time planning and superintending those beautiful ideas, which have transformed a bleak Northumbrian moor into an earthly paradise and made it almost as famous as his guns'. And, for Armstrong – as for his contemporaries at Biddulph, Bodnant and elsewhere – that meant rhodos, and more rhodos. In 1892 *The Gardeners' Magazine* reported that 'several hundred thousands (rhododendrons) have been planted ... forming impenetrable thickets and blooming so profusely as to light up the whole hillside with their varied colours'. Armstrong was sure that his labour of love had extended his life, observing 'I could not give the faintest idea of the pleasure it has afforded me ... it has been my very life'. By the time he died, in 1900 at the ripe old age of 90, he had planted over seven million trees which transformed 1000 acres of bleak hillside into a verdant and floral forest garden, complete with rhododendron maze.

Croome Park, *WORCESTERSHIRE* *
6TH EARL OF COVENTRY, 'CAPABILITY' BROWN

Most gardeners are natural enthusiasts, but some like George William, 6th Earl of Coventry are gardening zealots with, in his case, lots of ready cash available to spend on their obsession. As the first patron to recognize the skills of 'Capability' Brown, George and his wife were a perfect team – they were each zealous about different parts of the garden and so complemented one another perfectly. George had became heir to Croome after the unexpected death of his 23-year-old elder brother in 1744.

From 1748 onwards the development of Croome's house and garden became his life's work and according to Catherine Gordon's *The Coventrys of Croome* (2000) it appears that George's lifelong dedication to creating such a remarkable estate and landscape was born out of a bubbling cauldron of powerful emotions.

The deep grief at the loss of his brother could hint at the landscape as something of a memorial; but add to this feeling of loss a mixture of pride, a mild inferiority complex, great good taste, enthusiasm and wads of cash and it becomes clear how important to the successful outcome of the project was his designer. In 1750 he hired the 35-year-old

Brown, paying his commission in £5,000 instalments, small change compared to what Coventry spent making the plans become reality: some £400,000 over 61 years. Though he did realize that Brown wasn't doing badly out of the arrangement, for as early as 10th November 1752 he wryly wrote to a friend 'Mr Brown has done very well by me, and indeed I think he has studied both my Place and my Pocket, which are not always conjunctively the Objects of Prospectors'.

Brown's landscape quickly received universal plaudits and made Coventry the envy of the gardening elite. William Dean, the Head Gardener who wrote the first guide to the garden in 1824, just as the landscape was beginning to mature, describes:

'The drive beside the northern plantation around the lake where … the visitor is shut in, by the thick shades of large plantations … the borders of the lake … in the midst of scenery of more picturesque beauty and grandeur … an expanse of water, diversified with little verdant, wooded islands and hung all around with the thick foliage of overshadowing trees; which boldly rise from the sides or the summit of a sloping bank and reach down to the water's edge … in full luxuriance. It is a scene of calm delight, where all is serene and solemn. The stranger soon reaches a screen of rock work, a spar grotto and a water nymph … a copious spring is made to flow through her urn. Leaving the grotto the walk, winding among the woods which encompass the lake, affords, through an opening to the left, a good passing view of the house and admits from a seat placed round an oak, a perspective of the Panorama … hence to a handsome bridge to one of the islands.'

That's a rather impressive achievement, given that Coventry himself had described the site as being 'as hopeless a spot as any on the island'. But it wasn't only Brown's transformation of the unpromising marshland that made Croome so famous: by 1800 the garden was renowned as having a plant collection second only to Kew, amassed through the zealous activities of Coventry's second wife, Barbara. Some of the plants probably came from Badminton, since the Earl's relations included Lady Anne Somerset, the fourth daughter of the botanist Mary Capel, who had assembled a vast collection of plants at Badminton from sources across the world. Other plants came from nurseries and the estate's records from the 1770s show a continual influx of rare and unusual plants from France, Spain, the Falkland Islands, China and especially North America. In the grounds, 'must-sees' were the arboretum, which boasted more than 300 exotic trees and the Wilderness that, somewhat bizarrely, was famous for its truffles. The flower or Botanic Garden was filled with exotic and rare blooms and featured two hot houses dedicated to Cape plants from South Africa, as well as specimens from both the West and East Indies. The conservatory was filled with exceptionally rare Chinese plants and perhaps most cherished of all some of the earliest introductions from Botany Bay in Australia. Barbara must have had excellent contacts and a persuasive zeal: Botany Bay had only been named by Cooke and botanized by Banks as recently as April 1770 and the seeds Banks had gathered had gone to Kew.

Exbury, *HAMPSHIRE*
LIONEL DE ROTHSCHILD

Lionel de Rothschild (1808–79) would be glad to know that the gardens are now world famous, not least for the glorious collection of azaleas and rhododendrons. Like Lord Aberconway of Bodnant, Rothschild was both zealous and generous with regard to his plants. In the 1930s, Sir John Carew Pole of Antony House had visited Exbury and shown a great interest in the hybridizing experiments going on there. Rothschild suggested he make a list of his favourites, which Sir John did, then went home and thought no more about it. Several months later, just before Christmas, the stationmaster at North Road, Plymouth, rang to say he had two coal-trucks full of plants for Sir John, sent from Exbury.

Nymans Gardens, WEST SUSSEX *
LUDWIG MESSEL, JAMES COMBER

In the late 19th century Ludwig Messel (1847–1915) became addicted to collecting and hybridizing rhododendrons, building up a collection of 80 species and 50 named hybrids. Originally from a German Jewish family, Messel had moved to London in the 1860s where he founded his own stockbroking firm. As well as an enthusiasm for making money, Messel was both a competent artist and a music-lover, becoming friends with Gilbert and Sullivan. But it was his financial success that enabled him to buy Nymans in 1890 and, five years later, to secure the services of the 29-year-old James Comber (1866–1953) as Head Gardener. So began the first phase of intensive garden-making and a partnership that was to last for the rest of James's very long life.

Like many garden fanatics of the time (see Biddulph Grange, page 125), Messel was mad on rhododendrons and couldn't survive without the obligatory pinetum and arboretum. One of the first projects he and Comber undertook was to plant the pinetum, which contained no fewer than fifteen species of *Pinus*, following up with an arboretum shortly after. The gardens also contained a very early example of a heather garden – ericas and dwarf rhododendrons surrounded by a protective belt of *Pinus mugo*, a shrubby mountain pine. Messel would buy many of his exotic plants from the renowned Veitch nursery company, including magnolias and the sturdy Handkerchief tree (*Davidia involucrata*). The latter was one of the survivors of the devastating great storm of October 1987, during which Nymans lost a total of 486 mature trees: the restoration planting continues today (see Killerton, page 147).

Although an enthusiastic member of the Royal Horticultural Society (RHS), Messel refused to exhibit at their shows, much to the disappointment of Comber. But, with a true plant collector's zeal for one-upmanship, he did enter into friendly rivalries with his nearer neighbours – Gerald Loder at Wakehurst Place, Frederick Goodman at South Lodge, William Robinson at Gravetye and Arthur Soames at Sheffield Park.

In 1915 Nymans passed from Messel to his son, Leonard, and daughter-in-law, Maud. They lifted the ban on exhibiting and plants from Nymans began to regularly win prizes. Comber stepped up his breeding programme, especially with regard to camellias, rhododendrons and magnolias. One of his early successes was *Eucryphia* x *nymansensis* 'Nymansay', in fact a natural hybrid, that won the 1926 RHS Cory Cup for the year's best new hybrid and, two years later, a First Class Certificate. Other successful hybrids were created in the 1930s by crossing *Rhododendron decorum* 'Mrs Messel' (that Comber had created in the 1920s) with *R. griffithianum* (discovered by Hooker, see page 129).

Conveniently for Nymans, Comber's son, Harold, had undertaken several plant-hunting trips to South America in the 1920s. The gardens benefited from the seeds he brought back and 20 discoveries bear his name, including a new genus, *Combera*. Harold considered his best find to be what he called *Alstroemeria ligtu angustifolia* var. 'Vivid' (it is likely to have been *Alstroemeria presliana*). First shown in 1937, it is the ancestor of many brightly coloured alstroemerias now cultivated as a cut flower. In a slightly cruel twist of fate, given Comber's dedication, the most famous plants from Nymans, *Magnolia* x *loebneri* 'Leonard Messel' and M. 'Ann Rosse' were both raised in the 1950s by Comber's successor, Cecil Nice.

Sheffield Park Garden, *EAST SUSSEX* *
ARTHUR SOAMES

Arthur Soames (d.1934), who developed Sheffield Park from 1910–34, was an individualist. Over two decades he developed the grounds extensively but, rather than looking to the East, he looked West and collected North American native plants such as the Black gum or Tupelo (*Nyssa sylvatica*), Allegheny serviceberry (*Amelanchier laevis*), Highbush blueberry (*Vaccinium corymbosum*), scarlet oak (*Quercus coccinea*) and witch alder (*Fothergilla gardenii*). But Soames was not into collecting single specimens: instead his zeal was such that he'd plant dozens of each type. And it's the sheer numbers that create the year-round display for which the garden is so famous, in particular the profusion of rhododendrons and azaleas. After his death is 1934 his work was continued by his son Captain Granville Soames until the National Trust took over the property after its sale in 1954.

envy

'A desire to have something that is possessed by another. The other man's grass is always greener ...'

Just as making a garden or a plant collection could be an exercise in greed or zeal on the part of the proud owner, so often the result was – deliberate or not – a provocation to envy in others. In many cases, the expression of a passion by the owner was not was a calculated act of envy-engendering. However, in other cases, a deliberate display of one-upmanship was self serving, for the cause of envy simultaneously demonstrated the owner's good taste, purchasing power and status as a trend setter. To paraphrase George Orwell, some are always more equal than others, and the privileged sector of society within which the very wealthy gardened offered many different opportunities to engender envy. Be it the biggest collection of orchids, the largest bedding display, the most extensive range of glasshouses, the rarest new conifers, winning gold medals at flower shows, or employing a particularly ingenious Head Gardener whose new inventions or hybrid plants were showcased in your garden, all drew envious attention to one's garden.

Cliveden, *BUCKINGHAMSHIRE* *
GEORGE SUTHERLAND-LEVESON-GOWER, 2ND DUKE OF
SUTHERLAND, SIR CHARLES BARRY, JOHN FLEMING

In 1848, when the air outside Stoke became too foul at Trentham, the Duke of Sutherland (1786–1861) moved to Cliveden, calling once again upon the services of architect and garden designer Sir Charles Barry (1795–1880) to create a terraced garden and a stunning Italianate villa to go in it. Initially Sutherland had intended to simply revamp the existing house, but his plans were foiled when it burned to the ground during the restoration work (the second time this had happened during its long history). Barry (who also designed the Houses of Parliment) was the leading garden designer in the Italianate style, which had arisen a few years before in 1822.

John Claudius London (1783–1843) published his epic 1,200-page *Encyclopaedia of Gardening* (1822), which contained the first appraisal of garden history. The revelation that there were so many different historical styles from which to select an inspiration led inexorably to a gluttonous pick'n'mix approach where a dash of French was blended with a pinch of Dutch, a soupçon of Old English and a splash of Italian. This hotchpotch of styles came to be labelled 'Italianate', although it wasn't particularly redolent of Italian garden design. But it was a wonderful way of eliciting envy: as garden historian Richard Bisgrove eruditely observes in his book *The National Trust Book of the English Garden* (1990), the terraced gardens typical of Italianate design 'found favour equally with the patron, who could ostentatiously display his wealth and good taste, the architect, who could display his classical learning and geometrical inventiveness, and the gardener, who found, in the large, level terraces, the ideal site for exuberant displays of plants'.

The parterre at Cliveden was planted between 1851–53 by Head Gardener John Fleming (d.1883), who had also accompanied the Duke from Trentham. Fleming was a pioneer of bedding schemes and his bi-annual system boasted a spring show of over-wintered bulbs and biennials, planted in the autumn as a precursor to the summer's dazzling display of tender annuals. According to the *Journal of Horticulture and Cottage Gardener* in 1862, the parterre covered some 3½ acres: the vast triangular beds were edged with clipped privet and spruce, and partly filled with azaleas and rhododendrons with spaces left for hollyhocks, gladioli and foxgloves as well as summer and spring bedding. The spring bedding show alone used over 20,000 plants, as well as nearly 10,000 tulips. Simply maintaining the parterre required 60,000 plants a year.

William Robinson (1872): 'The great flower garden, one of the most repulsive examples of the extra formal school, thrusts itself in a rather awkward manner into the grand landscape'

This was not Fleming's only innovation, for in 1868 he created what *The Gardener's Chronicle* christened 'carpet bedding'. Their report went on to describe Fleming's monogram for Harriet Sutherland, where he had used *Arabis*, sempervivums, echeverias and sedums to pick out the Duchess's initials in different colours. The esteemed periodical enthused that the low growing plants and clipped foliage formed a surface as smooth and even as a Turkish carpet and suggested that everyone try it next year.

But the formal style did not receive universal approval. In 1872 William Robinson, the most vociferous advocate of a return to a more informal and natural approach to garden-making, proclaimed in the *The Garden* (which he both owned and edited): 'The great flower garden, one of the most repulsive examples of the extra formal school, thrusts itself in a rather awkward manner into the grand landscape.'

Croft Castle, *HEREFORDSHIRE* *

Spending wads of cash on the garden is one way to impress the envious crowd, but pedigree and oodles of history can do it too. In the grounds of Croft Castle there is a long avenue of exceptionally fine sweet or 'Spanish' chestnut trees, some with trunks over 8.5 metres (28 feet) in diameter. Legend has it that the trees are arranged to represent the battle formation lines of the ships of the Spanish Armada.

Dyrham Park, *SOMERSET* *
WILLIAM BLATHWAYT

William Blathwayt (1649–1717), who built himself a mansion at Dyrham and retired there in 1710 after a prominent career in the civil service and politics, wasn't adverse to using his position to make his garden the envy of his neighbours. As Auditor General for England's colonies in North America he was able to pull a few strings and was amongst the first to acquire the latest plant introductions. In 1695 he received seed of yucca, persimmon and *Magnolia virginiana* from Virginia and was also the recipient of a more bizarre consignment of 100 nightingales, two tomahawks not to mention a rather unenviable pair of live rattlesnakes!

Florence Court, *CO. FERMANAGH* *
WILLIAM WILLOUGHBY COLE, 1ST EARL OF ENNISKILLEN

One unbeatable claim of garden one-upmanship comes from Florence Court, home of the Irish or Florence Court yew (*Taxus baccata* var. *fastigiata*). While out hare coursing in the 1760s Mr George Willis found two plants growing in the wild; one he kept, the other he gave to William Willoughby Cole (Baron Mount Florence, later 1st Earl of Enniskillen). George's tree died in 1865, but the Earl's still thrives.

Fulham Palace, *LONDON*
HENRY COMPTON

Henry Compton (1632–1713), Bishop of London from 1676–1713, took full advantage of his missionary network to import an enviable variety of new plants from all over the world. The 17th-century writer and garden designer, Stephen Switzer recounts that Compton kept over 1,000 species in stoves (hot houses) in his Fulham gardens. Even before Queen Mary II's coronation in 1689, the Bishop's collection had grown so large that in the 1680s he had been forced to sell parts of it. Among those who purchased his 'cast offs' was Mary Capel, who developed her gardens at Badminton.

Glendurgan * and the Cornish Valley Gardens
THE FOX FAMILY

On the southern coast of Cornwall there are certain small valleys that enjoy a particularly munificent and gentle microclimate, the envy of all garden-makers. In the mid-19th century, when exotic plant collecting was all the rage, it soon became obvious that these sheltered valleys offered a sympathetic habitat, where semi-hardy and tender plants brought back from warmer climes could thrive alongside their hardier cousins. Made rich by maritime activities, the philanthropic Fox family was responsible for creating several of these verdant valley gardens, including Penjerrick (created by Robert Were Fox), Trebah (created by Charles Fox), and Glendurgan (created by Alfred Fox).

The gardens at Glendurgan were conceived in the 1820s with the maze planted in 1833, but the era of great plant collections began in the 1850s and lasted until World War I. These Cornish valley gardens became renowned both for the huge range of plants cultivated and the fact that many of these plants just could not be grown outdoors anywhere else in Britain. For an indication of just how floriferous the valley gardens were, in the late 19th century just four (Bosahan, Menabilly, Penjerrick, and Trebah) were between them successfully growing 392 different types of rare and unusual trees, shrubs, perennials and bulbs outdoors, all year round.

Popular plants in these gardens included Hooker's rhododendrons (the species, not the 'Hardy Hybrids'), which thrived on the acid soil and mild winters. There were also tender plants from South America such as *Azara* sp., *Berberidopsis corallina*, *Crinodendron hookerianum*, *Desfontainia spinosa*, *Embothrium coccineum*, and *Lapageria rosea* and from Australasia such as *Banksia integrifolia*, *Callistemon* sp., *Corokia* sp.,

Phormium tenax, *Pittosporum* spp., and *Podocarpus totara*. And it was in these mild Cornish gardens that the evergreen Tasmanian tree fern (*Dicksonia antarctica*) was first grown successfully, an example of an exotic plant that was not 'hunted' for deliberately. Many of the largest specimens still to be seen arrived in Falmouth harbour as ship's ballast and were casually tossed over board. They were left to rot on the foreshore, until someone noticed that one of the discarded 'logs' had sprouted large and elegant fronds (as it turned out, the usual way that the fern regenerates). At Penjerrick gardens, which in its heyday was probably the most fantastic of the valley gardens, there are today some massive tree ferns, over five metres (16 feet) high and two metres (6 feet) around.

Halton, *BUCKINGHAMSHIRE*
ALFRED VON ROTHSCHILD

After his father's death, Alfred von Rothschild (1842–1918) decided to build a weekend place in the country, on the site of the derelict family 'pile'. Alfred liked to impress his envious friends, but didn't much like to wait for things to grow so he insisted on the planting of full-grown trees and shrubs. It took a staff of 60 people to keep up with tending the thousands of plants and with meeting Alfred's demands: when he asked for roses in the conservatory, he meant 'fully grown'. He returned the next day to find a mass of 6 metre (20 foot) specimens had 'magically' appeared.

The ornate practice of 'carpet bedding' (see Cliveden, page 141) became a way of impressing envious visitors. The designs of the flowerbeds imitate the diamond-patterned flooring within the house, taking the 'carpet' aspect rather literally! Ernest Field, the Head Gardener to Alfred von Rothschild at Halton 'once heard it said that rich people used to show their wealth by the size of their bedding plant list: 10,000 for a squire, 20,000 for a baronet, 30,000 for an earl and 40,000 for a duke!' Rothschild, of course had 41,000! On a more modest scale, this style was enthusiastically taken up by Victorians, in both private gardens and municipal parks, as a way of imitating the 'gentry'. But in more recent years the fashion has waned, with a preference for more informal planting.

Hampton Court, *SURREY*
WILLIAM III & MARY II

With the accession of William and Mary (1662–94) to the British throne in 1689, plant envy received the royal seal of approval. Mary was an enthusiastic plant collector and gathered together plants from all over the world, either collected by her own plant hunters or brought back by the Dutch East India Company and displayed in three purpose-built hot houses, each 17 metres (55 feet) long. Mary's enviable collection of over 2000 different species was so big that she had her own in-house botanist, Dr Leonard Plukenet. Part of his job was to look after the 1000 orange trees, symbol of the House of Orange dynasty to which William belonged.

Killerton, *DEVON*
THOMAS ACLAND, JOHN VEITCH

The 19th-century habit of acquiring exotic plants from plant hunters was popular among the wealthy of the time, wanting to outdo each other with gardens filled with unusual, previously unknown plants. Desirable plants were acquired either by co-sponsoring an expedition or by buying them from commercial plant nurseries. The 19th century's most successful commercial nurseries was founded by John Veitch (1752–1839), a Scot from Jedburgh. His stroke of genius was to employ plant hunters to go on commercial expeditions to find plants only for his nurseries, making his stock eminently desirable.

In the 1770s, Veitch had been appointed Land Steward at Killerton in Devon by Sir Thomas Acland, 3rd Baronet (1722–85), and later went on to work for his son and heir, another Thomas. Veitch also rented land at nearby Lower Budlake and established a nursery selling mainly trees and shrubs. The business blossomed and John rented more land in 1810 before moving to larger premises at Mount Radford in 1832. This became the famous Exeter Nursery that, from 1837 was run by John's son, James. However, in 1853, in a move to compete with the great London-based nursery firms, James's son, also James, acquired the Royal Exotic Nursery in Chelsea. Eventually it became impractical to run both businesses side by side and in 1863 the Exeter and London branches became independent. The Veitch family name is commemorated today by hundreds of plant names, among them the palm genus *Veitchia*.

When the younger Thomas and his wife Lydia moved into Killerton in 1808, Lydia had asked John Veitch to make a 'proper' garden – something more enviable than the rather prosaic existing parkland of trees, grass, with itinerant deer that peered in through the dining room window. As a surprise for the couple on their return from honeymoon, John had built the Hermit's Hut. Allegedly, in the 1860s this rather strange wedding present became home to a single black bear, brought back from Canada. But it must have been an especially small or feeble animal: with its thatched roof, lattice windows, and flimsy walls the hut is more Hansel and Gretel than a sturdy bear cage. One of its more peculiar features is the somewhat macabre floor, constructed from carefully tessellated deer knucklebones. This was appositely described by Jane Loudon (wife of John Claudius) in her *Gardening for Ladies* (1840) as 'decidedly in bad taste'.

Even after John senior's death the Veitch family retained close connections with Killerton and many new introductions were first grown in the garden there. Such was the diversity and rarity of its plant collection that in the second half of the 19th century Killerton's gardens were highly envied by horticulturists. The thriving wellingtonias (*Sequoiadendron giganteum*), for example, were raised from the first packet of seed brought back from California by William

Lobb in December 1852: a year later the nursery were selling seedlings at two guineas each, extraordinarily expensive for the time.

Oxburgh Hall, *NORFOLK* *
SIR HENRY RICHARD PASTON-BEDINGFIELD, 6TH BARONET

In the 1800s the Italianate terrace or parterre was 'the' way to impress your friends (see Cliveden, page 141). The fully-restored parterre at Oxburgh Hall was created in 1845, in the latest and most fashionable way, for the appropriately-named Sir Henry Paston-Bedingfield (1800–62) and his wife Margaret. The design, one they first saw in Paris, was translated into elaborate box scroll work or *parterre de broderie*, filled with coloured gravels and crushed stones. In time, plants replaced the gravels and stones and the parterre became much admired. Next to the 15th-century Hall it must have looked as incongruous then as it does now and it makes for a strange historical juxtaposition today.

Waddesdon Manor, *BUCKINGHAMSHIRE* *
ALICE VON ROTHSCHILD, LORD ROTHSCHILD

At the turn of the 20th century the garden staff of over 100 at Waddesdon, inherited by Alice von Rothschild (1847–1992) in 1898, annually produced 50,000 plants for the flowering border, or parterre, set on its terrace below the house and fully restored by the National Trust and the Rothschild family. As with the garden as a whole, the parterre was maintained to the highest standards at all times – in the gardening press 'Waddesdon Standard' was synonymous with the highest excellence. Visiting Waddesdon, Frances, Countess of Warwick was most envious of this perfectionism. In her *Afterthoughts* (1931) she recalled how she had arrived there in a thunderstorm and was dismayed to find the masses of red pelargoniums had been beaten to a pulp by the weather. But the very next morning she looked out of her bedroom window to see an army of gardeners replanting the beds with new plants, brought from the glasshouses. By the end of breakfast the parterre had been completely rejuvenated! And, as might be expected, given this kind of attention to detail, Waddesdon had an enviable range of glasshouses. According to a former National Trust Chief Gardens Advisor, John Sales, the glasshouses at Waddesdon 'were extensive, with about fifty separate houses or sections, with the domed palm house as the main feature'.

If that wasn't enough to make the visitor jealous, there were the ornamental gardens, too. Perched on its hilltop overlooking the lovely Buckinghamshire countryside, Baron Ferdinand de Rothschild had wanted to create an appropriate setting when he first developed the property in the 1870s. As well as blithely shaving 3 metres (around 9 feet) of soil off Lodge Hill over an area of 10½ acres, in order to create a flat site for his French chateau-inspired manor house and its formal gardens, he provided the wider grounds with 'instant maturity', using a technique and horse-drawn equipment developed by William Barron to 'harvest' fully grown trees from the surrounding countryside and transplant them into the garden!

Whiteknights Park, *BERKSHIRE*
GEORGE SPENCER-CHURCHILL

Often, acquiring an object of envy also involves the expenditure of a great deal of money. In the gardening world, cultivating a large collection of rare and exotic plants has often been a status symbol of choice for the wealthy and George Spencer-Churchill, Marquis of Blandford (1766–1840), was no exception when it came to his garden at Whiteknights Park (now Reading University campus). George purchased the property in 1798 and, by the time he became the 5th Duke of Marlborough in 1817, had run up unenviable debts of £600,000 – most of which he had spent on enviable plants. Posh plants have always come with a high price

Posh plants have always come with a high price … as recently as the turn of the 20th century … a new orchid hybrid would regularly exceed 1,000 guineas

attached: even as recently as the turn of the 20th century, a single specimen of a new orchid hybrid would regularly exceed 1,000 guineas at auction – a sum that would have purchased a modest country house at that time.

gluttony

'Habitual greed or excess in eating.
                                    Overindulgence.'

The working walled gardens with their extensive range
of glasshouses and other functional buildings were not
generally on the garden tour offered to elegantly clad
visitors who genteelly perambulated around the
ornamental grounds. Yet the productive gardens were
integral and essential to the pride of the establishment.
For here, as well as the tender flowers raised for the
house, the conservatory and the summer bedding
displays, was grown a vast range of edible crops. Served
at the dining table (or exhibited at flower shows), not
only were these delicious fancies enjoyed by the family,
but to guests they also they offered another wonderful
example to demonstrate the horticultural prowess of the
establishment and occasional folly of the owner.

Beddington Park, *SURREY*
WILLIAM CECIL, 1ST LORD BURGHLEY, SIR FRANCIS CAREW

Lord Burghley (1520–98) of Hatfield House in Hertfordshire and Sir
Francis Carew (1530–1611) of Beddington in Surrey were the first two
nobleman to grow oranges in Britain, with trees brought from France in
1562. From this point on the orangery became a fashionable
adornment. In the winter it gave shelter for the valuable, but tender,
trees and, in summer, when the trees were placed out on the terraces,
the building could be used for other purposes, often for genteel

entertainment. There are notable orangeries at both Ham House and Blickling Hall.

For most owners, the orangery was as near as they got to 'hands on' engagement with the fruit and vegetables that were grown in their gardens, although they were quite happy to eat the vast range of produce available. An estate's productive gardens were like an embarrassing but wealthy relative: one knew they existed but most of the time one ignored them until they were the provisioner of largesse. 'Capability' Brown kept the kitchen garden out of sight of the house by placing it at a distance; 'Practicality' Repton brought it closer and hid it behind a shrubbery. Walled gardens were used as practical and discreet ways of raising tender, edible plants. The nearest many owners came to the production of their own fruit or veg was taking the credit when it won prizes at the local flower show!

> *An estate's productive gardens were like an embarrassing but wealthy relative: one knew they existed but most of the time one ignored them*

Belton House, *LINCOLNSHIRE* *

Belton House not only had a genteel orangery, but a rather gluttonous attitude to bedding plants – the terrace garden required 160,000 plants to be raised annually for the spring show alone. Just imagine the greenhouse space this required and the devastating consequences of an outbreak of *Phytophthora* (root rot)!

Castle Ward, *CO. DOWN* *
SIR JAMES CALDWELL, 4TH BARONET

Being able to serve out-of-season fruit, the earliest vegetables, or prize-winning pineapples were all indispensable ways of showing off one's gardening prowess at the dining table. However, for the true glutton, 'excessive' was the word: Sir James Caldwell (c.1722–84) gave a pointed account of his dining experience at Castle Ward in October 1772 and leaves the reader in no doubt that he was unimpressed:

'Lord Bangor received me with great cordiality … he also asked me to dine and stay all night. This was the greater compliment, as his house was full of company, and not quite finished … There was an excellent dinner … The second course of nine dishes [was] made out much in the same way. The cloth was taken away, and then the fruit a pine apple, not good; a small plate of peaches, grapes and figs (but a few), and the rest, pears and apples.'

Being able to serve out-of-season fruit, the earliest vegetables, or prize-winning pineapples were all indispensable ways of showing off one's gardening prowess

Even so, it had probably cost his host a pretty penny to come up with even this meagre display. As Walpole recorded earlier in the same century, the kitchen garden at Osterley Park cost some £1,400 a year to keep running.

Chatsworth, *DERBYSHIRE*
SIR JOSEPH PAXTON, DUKE OF DEVONSHIRE

Owners who wanted to feast on exotic or out of season fare were faced with the problem of how to grow it. Although the walled garden was the realm where all the specialist edible plants were planted out and raised, many had to be carefully sown and nurtured in dedicated greenhouses. In the 1800s Sir Joseph Paxton, Head Gardener to the Duke of Devonshire at Chatsworth (and most famous for his design for the Crystal Palace in 1851), made a fortune from his 'flat-pack' greenhouses. The range of different types of greenhouse (or glasshouse) offered, each type tailored to specific plants and conditions, was almost as great as the different range of crops grown.

Cliveden, *BUCKINGHAMSHIRE* *
HUGH LUPUS GROSVENOR, 1ST DUKE OF WESTMINSTER,
LADY NANCY ASTOR, 2ND VISCOUNTESS

As well as winning all the prizes at local and national garden shows, owners welcomed a chance to have their achievements praised in the horticultural press. In July 1877, for example, the *Gardeners' Chronicle* reported that the new range of glass erected at Cliveden, home of Hugh Lupus Grosvenor, 1st Duke of Westminster (1825–99), extended to some 32 different structures. The glasshouses particularly dedicated to raising edible crops included a late peach house, Muscat house, late vinery, early vinery, second vinery, apricot house, long vinery, fig house, melon range, a span-roofed pit used in spring in the raising of early vegetables, earliest house of peaches and nectarines, second peach house and a cucumber house.

By the 1930s, Cliveden had become home to the famous socialite and first woman MP to take her seat in the House of Commons. Nancy Astor (1879–1964) was noted for her flamboyant ways, which certainly didn't appeal to one frequent visitor, Sir Winston Churchill. Although as this infamous breakfast exchange indicates – she wasn't too fond of him either:

'Winston', said Lady Astor to Churchill, 'if I were married to you I'd put poison in your coffee'. 'Nancy', replied Churchill, 'if I were married to you, I'd drink it.'

> *In an admirably blatant display of floral gluttony, Lady Astor ordered the flower arrangements at Cliveden to be changed thrice daily*

In an admirably blatant display of floral gluttony, Lady Astor ordered the flower arrangements at Cliveden to be changed thrice daily: in the early morning, before lunch and again before dinner. As if that wasn't enough, a gardener was also dispatched daily to their London home, to do the flowers there.

Coombe Abbey, *WARWICKSHIRE*
9TH EARL OF COVENTRY & LADY BLANCHE CRAVEN

According to Catherine Gordon's book *Coventry's of Croome* (2000) an extravagant display took pride of place at the reception held in January 1865 to celebrate the union of the 9th Earl of Coventry and Lady Blanche Craven at Coombe Abbey. Proudly placed at the head of the dining table were six bunches of black grapes weighing a total of 36 pounds: they had been exhibited by the bride's father at Kew the previous Saturday, where they had won first prize.

Cragside House, *NORTHUMBERLAND* *
LORD ARMSTRONG

Lord Armstrong, ever the Victorian inventor, had an enviable array of glasshouses with a number of special gadgets of his own design. In the glasshouse dedicated to growing formally trained cherries, peaches, figs and other fruit trees, each tree was grown in a large stoneware pot, with the post arranged in tiers. Each pot sat on a turntable that was rotated regularly, so that all sides of the plant received equal amounts of sunlight, thus guaranteeing the maximum crop.

Dunster Castle, *SOMERSET* *

Dunster Castle claimed to have Britain's oldest lemon tree in its grounds, but sadly it died quite recently. But it must have produced copious amounts of fruit over the years. In the winter it was protected by a moveable frame and looked after with great care. Planted on the top terrace against the castle wall it was already well established by 1830 and described by *The Gardener's Magazine* as 'old' in 1842.

Gunnersbury Park, *LONDON*
LEOPOLD DE ROTHSCHILD

Leopold de Rothschild who inherited Ascott, in Buckinghamshire and later purchased Gunnersbury Park, was one gent who particularly enjoyed exhibiting the edible. At the 1912 Royal Horticultural Society Exhibition (the precursor of the Chelsea Flower Show), his exhibit of fruit trees from Gunnersbury Park covered 130 square metres (1,400 square feet) and had required 20 vans to transport it to the site. His passion for growing things was clearly one he hoped to impart to his offspring: at Ascott he had built for each of his sons 'a separate span-roof greenhouse, the plants in which are carefully attended personally by them during residence'.

Linton, *KENT*
LADY HOLMESDALE

A great diversity of tender specimens were brought to perfection in the greenhouses and beds of Linton, before going on display in the conservatory or Winter Gardens. Lady Holmesdale enjoyed a spot of gardening 'retail therapy', but who knows what her staff must have thought. On one shopping spree in the mid-19th century she spent £106 15s 0d just on new ferns at the Veitch nursery, while paying her Head Gardener a salary of £100 per annum.

On one shopping spree ...
[Lady Holmesdale, of Linton]
spent £106 15s 0d just on
new ferns ... while paying her
Head Gardener a salary of
£100 per annum.

Penrhyn Castle, *GWYNEDD* *
EDWARD SHOLTO DOUGLAS-PENNANT, 3RD BARON PENRHYN

An 1895 account of a visit to Penrhyn Castle, reported in the *Journal of Horticulture and Cottage Gardener*, gave a flattering account of the productive garden and listed some of the crops grown. Raised within the greenhouses were six types of grape including 'Foster's Seedling' and 'Lady Downe's Seedling' (both of which had been bred by Thomas Foster, Head Gardener for nearly 40 years at Beningbrough Hall). There were also four types of peaches and nectarines, three types of pineapple and Brown Turkey fig trees, the largest of which measured 21 metres (70 feet) or more in width. Melons were harvested from April well into the autumn with Penrhyn Seedling 'largely depended upon and well spoken of'. Other crops included 'salading', indoor and outdoor tomatoes, potatoes (probably grown under cover), mushrooms, morello cherries, gooseberry, blackcurrants and passion fruit (*Passiflora quadrangularis*).

Such produce would be destined for the dining table in the country house, or meticulously packed and sent up to the town house during the 'season' or to wherever it was needed. In the 1920s the 3rd Baron Penrhyn (1864–1927) was chief official of the Jockey Club and travelled the country from one race meeting to another. According to Norman Thomas, who worked in the gardens for two years from 1924, his needs were few:

> 'Fresh fruit, vegetables and flowers had to be at the place he was visiting one day prior to his arrival … Grapes had to arrive at their place of destination with their bloom intact. Peaches, figs and similar fruit required special attention in their packing. All fruit was placed in special paper with wool and wood wool surrounding them, they were then placed in special boxes … (In) 1926 there was a National Strike – sending goods by rail was not possible and only a few ounces were allowed through the post. To get over this difficulty each tomato was sent separately. One tomato was wrapped in cotton wool and put into a small cardboard box, each box with an addressed label. Scores and scores of these boxes were sent by this method. They arrived at their place of destination in perfect condition.'

Petworth House, *WEST SUSSEX* *
HENRY WYNDHAM, 2ND LORD LECONFIELD

Although the costs of running a productive fruit and vegetable garden could be high, this didn't prevent some owners indulging in rather extravagant and conspicuous consumption. In the late 19th century, the kitchen garden at Petworth was the location for a spectacular exhibition of gluttonous folly, brought on by pride. As John Wyndham, Lord Egremont, noted in his memoirs, Henry, 2nd Lord Leconfield (1830–1901) was not one to be out done by a guest. When, over dessert, said guest pompously observed that while imported bananas were quite adequate, in matters of taste they simply did not match up to that of a fruit picked straight from the tree. Saying nothing at the time this statement loaded with one-upmanship and a slight slur on his hospitality, hit a raw nerve with his Lordship. For the next morning the Head Gardener was summoned and summarily dispatched to Kew to learn all there was to be learned about banana cultivation. Back at Petworth a special greenhouse was duly erected and its inhabitants nurtured with tender care. At last the great day came when said fruit was proclaimed ripe, harvested, and served to his Lordship with due pomp and ceremony. Taking up a golden knife and fork his Lordship peeled it, cut a slice and tasted. With everyone from family to servants agog, he 'flung dish, plate, knife, fork and banana on to the floor and shouted, "Oh God, it tastes just like any other damn banana!"' So banana cultivation at Petworth came to a rapid end, and it may be that his single banana was the most expensive ever eaten, for the price of this Lordly pride was estimated to be a staggering £3,000.

bibliography

GARDEN HISTORIES

Bisgrove, R., *The National Trust Book of the English Garden* (London, Viking, 1990)

Hobhouse, P., *The Story of Gardening* (London, Dorling Kindersley, 2002)

Uglow, J., *A Little History of British Gardening* (London, Chatto & Windus, 2004)

BOOKS

Andrews, C Bruyn (ed.), *The Torrington Diaries; Containing the tours through England and Wales of The Hon. John Byng (later fifth Viscount Torrington) between the years 1781 and 1794* (London, Eyre & Spottiswoode, 1938)

Antony, J, *Joseph Paxton* (Aylesbury, Shire Publications Ltd, 1985) The Paxton Society (csasip2.gold.ac.uk/paxton/resources.html) has a 1973 edition

Betham-Edwards, M (ed.), *The Autobiography of Arthur Young.* (London, Smith, Elder & Co, 1898)

Blacker, M R, *Flora Domestica. A History of Flower Arranging 1500–1930* (London, National Trust, 2000)

Brown, J, *Sissinghurst: Portrait of a Garden* (London, Weidenfeld Nicolson, 1998)

Bruce, H J, *Silken Dalliance* (London, Constable, 1946)

Colquhoun, K, *A Thing in Disguise: The Visionary Life of Joseph Paxton* (London, Fourth Estate, 2003)

Cooper, P M, *The Story of Claremont* (London, West, 1979)

Daniels, S, *Humphry Repton* (New Haven and London, Yale University Press, 1999)

Dashwood, Sir Francis, *The Dashwoods of West Wycombe* (London, Aurum Press, 1987)

Desmond, R, *Kew: A History of the Royal Botanic Gardens* (London, The Harvill Press, 1995)

Lord Egremont, *Wyndham and Children First* (London, Macmillan, 1969)

Elliott, B, *Victorian Garden* (London, B T Batsford Ltd, 1986)

Gill, C, *The Park and Garden of Antony House* (unpublished manuscript, c.1987)

Gordon, C, *Coventry's of Croome* (Chichester, Phillimore & Co. Ltd, 2000)

Hadfield, M, *A History of British Gardening* (London, Spring Books, 1969)

Hadfield, M, *British Gardeners: a biographical dictionary* (London, Zwemmer, 1980)

Harvey, J, *Mediaeval Gardens* (London, B T Batsford, 1981)

Hillier, *The Hillier Manual of Trees and Shrubs*, 6th edition (Newton Abbot, David & Charles, 1996)

Honour, H & Fleming, J, *The Visual Arts: A History*, 6th edition (London, Prentice Hall, 2002)

Hoyles, M, *The Story of Gardening* (London, Journeyman Press, 1991)

Hunt, J D, *William Kent Landscape Garden Designer* (London, A Zwemmwe Ltd, 1987)

Jellicoe, G *et al.*, *The Oxford Companion to Gardens* (Oxford, Oxford University Press, 1986

Kellaway, D (ed.) *The Illustrated Virago Book of Women Gardeners* (London, Virago, 1997)

Lasdun, S, *The English Park* (London, Andre Deutsch, 1991)

Lawson, W, *A New Orchard And Garden with The Country Housewife's Garden: a Facsimile edition with an introduction by Malcolm Thick* (Totnes, Prospect Books, 2003)

Lees-Milne, J, *Ancestral Voices: Diaries 1942–1943* (London, Chatto & Windus, 1975)

Lees-Milne, J, *Caves of Ice* (London, John Murray, 1996)

Lees-Milne, J, *Midway on the Waves* (London, John Murray, 1996)

Lees-Milne, J, *Prophesying Peace* (London, Faber & Faber, 1977)

Lucy, M E, *Mistress of Charlecote: The Memoirs of Mary Elizabeth Lucy* (London, Victor Gollancz, 1987)

McLean, B, *George Forrest Plant Hunter* (Suffolk, Antique Collectors' Club, 2004)

Mannix, D, *The Hell Fire Club* (London, New English Library, 1967)

Morgan, J & Richards, A, *A Paradise out of a Common Field* (London, Century, 1990)

Musgrave, T, Gardner, C & Musgrave, W, *The Plant Hunters* (Ward Lock, 1997)

National Trust Property Guides (Much information is to be found about individual gardens in the guides published by the National Trust)

O'Brien, J & Guinness, D, *Great Irish Houses and Castles* (London, Orion Publishing Co, 1993)

Paston-Williams, S, *The Art of Dining* (London, National Trust, 1995)

Phibbs, J, *Wimpole Hall, Cambridgeshire* (London, National Trust, 1979) (Unpublished National Trust Survey)

Reeves-Smyth, T J C, *Florence Court: Inventory* (London, National Trust, 1987) (Unpublished National Trust Survey)

Ridgeway, C (ed.), *William Andrews Nesfield: An Introduction to His Life and Work* (York, Institute of Advanced Architectural Studies, 1996)

Salwey, Jasper, *Guide to Rothbury* (1913)

Sampson, Rev G V, *Statistical Survey of the County of Londonderry* (1802)

Strong, R, *The Renaissance Garden in England* (London, Thames & Hudson, 1979)

Strong, R, *The Artist and the Garden* (London and Newhaven, Yale University Press, 2000)

Stroud, D, *Capability Brown* (London, Faber & Faber, 1984)

Stuart, D, *The Garden Triumphant* (London, Viking, 1988)

Thacker, C, *The History of Gardens* (London, Croome Helm Ltd, 1979)

Thomas, G S, *Gardens of the National Trust* (London, Weidenfeld & Nicholson, 1979)

Throsby, J, *The History and Antiquities of the Town and County of the Town of Nottingham; containing the whole of Thoroton's account of that place and what is valuable in Deering* (Nottingham, Burbage & Stretton, 1795)

Tilden, P, *True Remembrances: the memoirs of an architect* (London, Country Life, 1954)

Tuck, C, *Landscapes and Desire* (Stroud, Sutton Publishing, 2003)

Turner, R, *Capability Brown and the Eighteenth Century English Landscape* (Chichester, Phillimore & Co. Ltd, 1999)

Warwick, Frances Countess of, *Afterthoughts* (London, Cassell & Co Ltd, 1931)

Waterson, M (ed.), *The Country House Remembered: Recollections of Life Between the Wars* (London, Routledge Kegan & Paul, 1985)

Waterson, M, *The Servants' Hall: A Domestic History of Erddig* (London, Routledge Kegan & Paul, 1980)

Willes, M, *Country House Estates* (London, National Trust, 1996)

Willis, P, *Charles Bridgeman and the English Landscape Garden* (Newcastle-upon-Tyne, Elysium Press, 2002)

Wilson, A N, *The Victorians* (London, Arrow Books, 2003)

Wodehouse, P G, *Blandings Castle* (London, Herbert Jenkins, 1935)

PERIODICAL ARTICLES

Adshead, D, 'A Modern Italian Loggia At Wimpole Hall', *Georgian Group Journal,* 10:150–63 (2000)

Chappell, H, 'Rememberance of England Past', *Independent on Sunday,* 22 May 1994

Cheshire Life, 'Oranges and Lemons'

Chessum, S, 'Claremont revisited: Uncovering the Duke of Newcastle's garden', *Apollo*

Cornforth, J, 'Basildon House, Berkshire – III', *Country Life,* 13 September 1979, 758–759.

Country Life No. 321, 'Coughton Court, Warwickshire', 30 March, 1918

Country Life, 'Coughton Court, Warwickshire', 19 May 1978, pp.96

Country Life, 31 May 1990, 155.

Country Life, 8 December 1900, 738.

Country Life 'Munstead House', 8 December 1900

Eyres, Patrick, 'The Invisible Pantheons of Thomas Hollis at Stowe and in Dorset', *New Arcadian Journal* 55/56 (2003) pp45–70

Festing, Sally, 'Menangeries and the Landscape Garden', *Journal of Garden History,* Volume 8, No. 4 (1988), pp.109–112

The Garden, 'The Gardens of England – Cragside', 12 October 1872, p.315

The Garden History Society News, 60 'Letter from Mrs Vivienne Lewis, Taunton', (Autumn 2000), p.24

Garden Life, 24 June 1905, 213–5.

Gardeners' Chronicle, 'Claremont Park', 29 April 1882

Gardeners' Chronicle, Volume 8, 'Cliveden', 21 July 1877, pp.69–70

Gardeners' Chronicle, Volume 19, 'Ascot', 8 February 1896, pp156–6 and 173

Gardeners' Chronicle, Volume 4, 'Belton Park, Grantham', 3 November 1888, p506

Gardeners' Chronicle, Volume 17, 'Cliveden', 22 June 1895, pp765–766

Gardeners' Chronicle, 'Newcastle-upon-Tyne', (1894)

The Gardening World Illustrated, Volume I, 'A Gardener's Bothy', 13 December 1884, 233

Gilkes, K, 'Clandon Park', *Lady*, 29 April 1971

Hooke, D, 'The Warwickshire Arden: The Evolution and Future of an Historic Landscape', *Landscape History* 10, 1980

'Hypomnemata', unpublished manuscript, (London, British Library, Add.Ms.6230)

Jackson-Stops, G, 'Formal Garden Designs for Cliveden', *National Trust Year Book* (1976–77)

Jackson-Stopes, Gervase, 'Dunham Massey, Cheshire II', *Country Life*, (1981), p1666

Journal of the Royal Horticultural Society 60/12

Public Parks at Newcastle-upon-Tyne, Volume 15, (1894), pp. 748–51 and 814–5

Royal Oak Newsletter, 'Restoring the Magic – Cragside Gardens', Summer 2001, p1–5

Sales, J. 'High Victorian Horticulture: the Garden at Waddesdon'. pp.77–89

Scribbler, 'Penrhyn Castle', *Journal of Horticulture and Cottage Gardener*, New Series Volume 31:131, (1895)

Text of a Paper for the Collecing Sculpture in Early Modern Symposium, National Gallery of Art, Washingon, 7–8 February 2003

Warwick:Warwickshire County Record Office 'Lady Newdigate's journal of 1748'

Wheeler, R, *Sir Frances Dashwood of West Wycombe Park, Buckinghamshire as a Collector of Ancient and Modern Sculpture*, Buckinghamshire County Gardens Trust Newsletter

Wheeler, Richard, 'Fay ce que Voudras, or Pro Magne Charta', *New Arcadian Journal* 49/50, (2000), pp1–160

GENERAL REFERENCE WEBSITES

How Much Is That Worth Today? Comparing the purchasing power of money in Great Britain from 1264 to 2005: www.eh.net/hmit/ppowerbp/

index

Figures in *italics* indicate captions

Aberconway, Henry McLaren, 2nd
    Lord 102, 131, 136
Acland, Lady Lydia 148
Acland, Sir Thomas, 3rd Baronet
    147
Acland, Sir Thomas, 5th Baronet
    148
Adam, Robert 66
Aislabie, John 97–8
Aislabie, William 98
Alexandra, Queen 32, 39
Alfred the Great 48
All England Lawn Tennis and
    Croquet Club, Wimbledon,
    London 122
Allen, Ralph 45–6
Amory, Lady (Joyce Wethered) 118
Anglesey, Lord and Lady 131
Anne, Queen 82
Anson, Admiral Lord 18
Antony, Cornwall 109, 136
Ark Club, London 37
Arley Hall, Cheshire 128
Arlington Court, Devon 26, 94
Armstrong, William George, 1st
    Lord 32, 132–4, 157
Arne, Thomas 43
Artois, Comte d' 32
Ascott, Buckinghamshire 27, 157
Astor, 3rd Viscount 61
Astor, Lady Nancy, 2nd Viscountess
    156
Astor family 102
Attingham Park, Shropshire 9, 94
Augustine, St 70

Baccelli, Giovanna 119
Baddesley Clinton, Warwickshire

80–81, 110
Badminton, Gloucestershire 136, 145
Baillie Scott, Mackay Hugh 21
Balfour, Arthur, 1st Earl of 121
Ballyscullion, Co. Derry 13
Bambridge, Elsie 25
Bambridge, George 25
Bangor, Lord 154
Banks, Sir Joseph 128, 136
Barron, William 151
Barry, Sir Charles 141
Basildon Park, Berkshire 111–12
Bateman, James 125–30
Bateman, Maria 125–30
Batemans, East Sussex 27–8, 30
Bath, Lord 31–2
Beddington Park, Surrey 152–3
Belton House, Lincolnshire 123, 153
Beningbrough Hall, North Yorkshire
    158
Benthall Hall, Shropshire 124–5
Berwick, Thomas, 8th Lord 94
Berwick of Attingham, Noel Hill,
    1st Lord 9
Betjeman, John 21–2
Bickersteth, Miss 63, 64
Biddulph Grange Garden,
    Staffordshire 125–30, 133
Bisgrove, Richard 141
Blandford, George Spencer-
    Churchill, Marquis of (later 5th
    Duke of Marlborough) 151
Blathwayt, William 144
Blenheim Palace, Woodstock,
    Oxfordshire 49–50, 57
Blickling Hall, Norfolk 30, 102
Bodiam Castle, East Sussex 40–41
Bodnant Court, Conwy, North
    Wales 102, 131, 133, 136
Boevey, Catherine 54

Bosahan gardens, Cornwall 145
Bowes, George 64
Bowes, Mary Eleanor 64, 65
Bowes-Lyon, John, 9th Earl of
  Strathmore 64
Bradshaw, Mr (Head Gardener,
  Waddesdon Manor) 150
Braker, Samuel 100
Bridgeman, Charles 23, 31, 45,
  49–51, 68, 115
Bristol, Frederick Augustus Hervey,
  4th Earl of 12–14
Bristol High Cross 48
Brock, Edmund 38, 39
Brome, John 110
Brompton Park Nursery, Kensington,
  London 82
Brookfield, Jane Octavia 59
Brookfield, Rev. William Henry 59
Brown, Lancelot 'Capability' 10, 11,
  16–19, 22–5, 45, 47, 53, 85,
  134–5, 153
Buckingham, George Villiers, 2nd
  Duke of 60, 61
Buckingham Palace, London 32
Budding, Edwin Beard 115
Burghley, William Cecil, 1st Lord
  152
Burghley House, Lincolnshire 88
Burlington, Richard Boyle, 3rd Earl
  of 51–2
Burnet, Bishop 43, 44
Bush, George W. 81
Bute, John Stuart, 3rd Earl of 75,
  78–9

Caldwell, Sir James, 4th Baronet 154
Canons Ashby, Northamptonshire
  81–2, 82
Capel, Mary (Duchess of Beaufort)
  136, 145
Carew, Sir Francis 152
Carew, Richard 109
Carew, Sir Richard 109
Caroline, Queen (wife of George II)
  51

Caroline, Queen (wife of George IV)
  111
Carteret, Lord 31–2
Castle Ward, Co. Down 10, 154
Catesby, Robert 41, 113
Catherine the Great, Empress of
  Russia 23–4
Cecil, Lord Hugh 37
Chambers, Sir William 11
Champernowne, Sir Arthur 109
Charlecote Park, Warwickshire 10,
  63, 152
Charles I, King 44, 118
Charles II, King 44, 44
Chartwell, Kent 84–5, 112
Chastleton House, Oxfordshire
  41–2, 113, 115
Chatsworth, Derbyshire 128, 155
Chatterton, Georgina, Lady 80, 81
Chelsea Flower Show, London 157
Chichester, Rosalie 26, 94
Child, Robert 66, 93
Child, Sarah Ann 66
Chiswick House, London 52
Churchill, Charles 75
Churchill, Clemmie (Clementine;
  Baroness Spencer-Churchill) 84
Churchill, Sir Winston 84, 85, 112,
  113, 156
Churt, Kent 85
Claremont Landscape Garden,
  Surrey 11, 31–2, 50, 85–6,
  114–15
Clevedon Court, Somerset 59
Clifford, Rosamond 57
Clive, Robert, Baron Clive of Plassey
  11, 85–6
Cliveden, Buckinghamshire 43,
  50, 60–61, 102, 116, 141–3,
  155–6
Clumber Park, Nottinghamshire 62,
  100–101
Cobham, Lady 123
Cobham, Richard Temple, 1st
  Viscount 49, 51, 52, 53, 68, 73,
  74, 76, 77, 123

Colchester, Maynard 54–5
Colchester, Maynard (nephew) 55
Colly, Thomas 128
Comber, Harold 138
Comber, James 137, 138
Compton, Henry, Bishop of London
    144–5
Cooke, Edward 126
Cooke, James 136
Coombe Abbey, Warwickshire 156
Cordell, Sir William 120
Cory, Reginald 104, 105
Coughton Court, Warwickshire 96,
    110
Coventry, 9th Earl of 156
Coventry, Barbara, Countess of 136
Coventry, George William, 6th Earl
    of 11, 134–6
Coventry, George William, 9th Earl
    of 117
Cragside House, Northumberland
    32, 101, 132–4, 157
Craven, Lady Blanche 156
Croft Castle, Herefordshire 143
Croome Park, Worcestershire 11,
    117, 134–6

Dalyngrigge, Sir Edward 40–41
Darwin, Charles 129
Dashwood, Francis, 2nd Baronet
    (later 15th Baron le Despencer)
    71–9
Dashwood, Francis, 11th Baronet 79
Dashwood, Lady Sarah (née Ellys)
    76, 79
Dean, William 135
Dering, Edward Heneage 80, 81
Devizes Castle, Wiltshire 101
Devonshire, Duke of 155
Disraeli, Benjamin 88, 113
Disraeli, Mary Anne 88
Divan Club 74
Doddington, George Bubb (later
    Lord Melcombe Regis) 75, 77
Doe, Robert 98
Donowell, John 77

Douglas, David 128
Downhill Estate and Mussenden
    Temple, Co. Londonderry 12–14
Drake, Sir Francis 115
Dryden, Edward 81–2, 82
Dryden, Erasmus Henry 81
Dryden, Sir Henry 81
Dryden, John 81
Dryden family 81
Dudmaston, Shropshire 117
Dufferin, Frederick, Lord 37
Dunham Massey, Cheshire 14–15
Dunster Castle, Somerset 157
Dyffryn, near Cardiff 104
Dyrham Park, Somerset 144
Dysart, Elizabeth 43–5

Edward I, King 119
Edward II, King (as Prince Edward)
    120
Edward VII, King 32, 94
Egerton, Lord Allan 99
Egerton, Lord Maurice 99
Egremont, John Wyndham, 4th Lord
    19, 160–61
Elizabeth, Queen, the Queen Mother
    39, 64
Elizabeth I, Queen 70–71, 86, 87, 91,
    120
Elliott, Brent 127
Elton, Sir Charles 59
Enclosure Acts (1760s) 9, 15
Enniskillen, William Willoughby
    Cole, 1st Earl of 144
envy 140–51
Erddig, Northumberland 33
Esher, Lord 71
Evelyn, John 43
Exbury, Hampshire 131, 136
Exeter Nursery, Mount Radford,
    Devon 148
Eywood, Herefordshire 63–4

Fairburn, Mr (nurseryman) 128
Faud, King of Egypt 37
Fawkes, Guy 91

Felbrigg Hall, Norfolk 15, 123
Fenstanton, Huntingdonshire 16–17
Ferrers, Marmion Edward 80, 81
Ferrers, Undine 81
Field, Ernest 146
Flaxley Abbey, Gloucestershire 54
Fleming, John 142
Florence Court, Co. Fermanagh 144
Foot, Jesee 65
Forrest, George 104–5, 131
Fortune, Robert 126, 132
Foster, Thomas 158
Fountains Abbey, Yorkshire 98
Fox family (Cornwall) 145
Franklin, Benjamin 72
Frary, Robert 123
Frederick, Prince of Wales 43, 75, 116
Frogmore, Windsor Castle estate,
    Berkshire 101
Fryberg, Sir Bernard 131
Fulham Palace, London 144–5

Gainsborough, Thomas 119
Gaveston, Piers 120
generosity 26–39
George I, King 31, 49
George II, King 31, 50–51, 53
George III, King 16, 48, 79
Gibb, James 52
Gibside, Northumberland 64–5
Gilpin, William 98
Glendurgan and the Cornish Valley
    Gardens 145–6
Glover, Richard 70
gluttony 152–61
Goodman, Frederick 138
Goodyear, Charles 121
Gordon, Catherine 134
Grace, W G 122
Gravetye Manor, West Sussex 138
greed 8–25
Grenville, George 78
Grenville, Richard 53, 78
Greville, Hon. Ronald 94
Greville, Mrs Ronald 94, 95
Grey, George 65

Grey, Jemima, Marchioness of 23, 24
Guarini, Giovanni Battista 68
Gunby Hall, Lincolnshire 17
Gunnersbury Park, London 157

Hallam, Henry 59
Halton, Buckinghamshire 146–7
Ham House, Surrey 43–5, 152
Hampton Court Palace, Surrey 54,
    82, 121, 147
Hardwick Hall, Derbyshire 86–7, 91,
    118
Hardwicke, Charles Philip Yorke,
    5th Earl of 25
Hardwicke, Philip Yorke, 1st Earl 23
Hardwicke, Philip Yorke, 2nd Earl 23
Hatfield House, Hertfordshire 152
Heathcoat, John 36
Heathcoat Amory, Sir John 36
Hell Fire Club 74
Hellfire Caves, West Wycombe 74–5
Henry II, King 57
Henry VIII, King 81, 115, 121
Hibberd, James Shirley 129–30
Hidcote Manor, Gloucestershire
    102–5
Hoare, Henry, II 47–8, 67
Hogarth, William 75
Holbeache House, Staffordshire 41
Holdenby House, Northamptonshire
    88
Holmesdale, Lady 158
Home House, near Worthing, West
    Sussex 130
Hooker, Sir Joseph 125, 129, 130,
    132, 138, 145
Hughenden Manor,
    Buckinghamshire 88
Hyde–Parker, Lady 106–7

Ickworth, Suffolk 13, 14
Ingram, 'Cherry' 104
Ivanov, Yevgeny 'Eugene' 61

James II, King of Scotland 118
Jefferson, Thomas 81

Jekyll, Gertrude 39
Johnson, Arthur Tysilio 104
Johnston, Lawrence 102, 103–5
Jones, Arthur, I 42
Jones, Henry 42
Jones, Walter 41–2

Keeler, Christine 61
Kent, William 48, 51–2, 53, 68, 69
Kew Gardens, Surrey (Royal Botanic
    Gardens) 116, 129, 136, 156, 160
Killerton, Devon 147–9
Killigrew, Harry 61
King, Sir John Dashwood 79
King, Thomas 101
Kingdon-Ward, Frank 131
Kip, Johannes 54, 55
Kipling, Caroline (Carrie) 28, 30
Kipling, Rudyard 25, 27–8, 28, 30
Kirby Hall, Northamptonshire 88
Knightshayes Court, Devon 36, 118
Knole, Kent 34, 35, 46, 119–20
Knutsford Boys' Club, Cheshire 99
Knypersley Hall, Staffordshire 127

Langdale, Lady 63–4
Langdale, Lord 63
Lauderdale, John Maitland, Duke of
    43–4
Leconfield, Charles Wyndham, 3rd
    Lord 19
Leconfield, Henry, 2nd Lord 160
Lees-Milne, James 20, 85, 103–4
Leggett, Thomas 9
Leinster, Duke of 16
Leoni, Giacomo 116
Lichfield, Thomas Anson, 1st Lord
    74
Limerick, Lord 31–2
Lindley, Dr 128
Lindsay, Nancy 102–3
Lindsay, Norah 38, 102–3
Linton, Kent 158
Lloyd, Robert 75
Lloyd George, David 85
Lobb, William 126, 148–9

Loder, Gerald 138
London, George 81–2
Londonderry, Charles Vane-
    Tempest-Stewart, 7th Marquess
    of 37
Londonderry, Edith, Marchioness of
    37, 38–9
Londonderry House, London 37
Londonderry's (at Mount Stewart)
    102
Lothian, Lady 30
Lothian, Lord 102
Loudon, Jane 148
Loudon, John Claudius 141, 148
love 80–99
Lucy, George 10
Lucy, Mary Elizabeth 63, 64
Ludlow, Frank 131
lust 56–79
Lyveden New Bield,
    Northamptonshire 88–9, 96

Mannix, Daniel P. 77
Marlborough, Sarah, Duchess of 50
Mary I, Queen 38
Mary II, Queen 54, 144, 147
Mary, Queen 20
Massingberd, Peregrin Langton 17
Maw, George 124–5
Maxwell, Sir Herbert 38
Medmenham Abbey,
    Buckinghamshire 75
Melford Hall, Suffolk 106–7, 120
Menabilly gardens, Cornwall 145
Messel, Leonard 138
Messel, Ludwig 137–8
Messel, Maud 138
Mewes and Davis (Charles Mewes
    and Arthur Joseph Davis,
    architects) 95
Millington & Sons 112
Milton Abbas, Dorset 18
Milton Abbey, Dorset 18
Milton, Lord 18
Monk's House, East Sussex 90
Monks of Medmenham 74

Monreith, Wigtownshire 38
Montacute House, Somerset 91–2
Moor Park, Herefordshire 18
Morrison, James 111
Morrison, Major James Archibald 112
Mount Stewart House, Co. Down 37–9, 102
Mussenden, Frideswide 13
Mussenden Temple see Downhill Estate

National Trust 7, 20, 22, 25, 43, 45, 55, 71, 79, 95, 102, 103, 139, 149
Newcastle-Under-Lyme, Kathleen, 7th Duchess of 100
Newcastle-under-Lyme, Thomas, 1st Duke of 31
Nice, Cecil 138
Nicolson, Harold 46, 47
Nugent, Major Andrew 10
Nymans Garden, West Sussex 67, 137–8

Old Bowling Green Club, Southampton 115
Oliver, Dr William 117
Orford, Earl of 32
Orkney, George Hamilton, Earl of 116
Orpen, Rebecca Dulcibella 80, 81
Osborne House, Isle of Wight 114
Osterley Park, Middlesex 66, 93, 121–2, 154
Oxburgh Hall, Norfolk 149
Oxford, Edward Harley, 2nd Earl of 23

Paston-Bedingfield, Sir Henry, 6th Baronet 149
Paston-Bedingfield, Lady Margaret 149
Paxton, Sir Joseph 99, 155, 161
Penjerrick gardens, Cornwall 145, 146
Penrhyn, Edward Sholto Douglas-Pennant, 3rd Baron 159

Penrhyn Castle, Gwynedd 158–9
Pepys, Samuel 60
Petworth House, Sussex 19, 121, 160–61
Phelips, Sir Edward 91
Phillips, James 33
Plas Newydd, Llanfairpwll, Anglesey 131
Plukenet, Dr Leonard 147
Pole, Sir John Carew 136
Pole-Carew, Reginald 109
Polesden Lacy, Surrey 94–5
Pomfret, Mr (Head Gardener, Melford Hall) 106–7
Pope, Alexander 45, 51, 52, 53
Portland, Winnie, Duchess of 101
Potter, Thomas, MP 75
pride 40–55
Prior Park, Somerset 45–6
Pritchard, Thomas 33
Profumo, John 61

Queensberry, Duke of 75

Rabelais, François 72
Radnor, Charles Robartes, 2nd Earl of 22, 23
Rand, Conway, vicar of Stowe 69
Rapin, René 47
Repton, Humphry 79, 99
Revett, Nicholas 74
Reynolds, Sir Joshua 119
Rhode, Eleanour Sinclair 38
Richmond Park, Surrey 32
Robinson, William 138, 142–3
Rock, Joseph 131
Rosemoor, north Devon 104
Ross, Sir John 38
Rostrevor House, Co. Down 38
Rothschild, Alfred de 146
Rothschild, Alice 149, 150
Rothschild, Baron Ferdinand de 150–51
Rothschild, Leopold de 27, 157
Rothschild, Lionel de 131, 136
Royal Exotic Nursery, Chelsea 148

Royal Horticultural Society (RHS) 39, 100, 102, 131, 137, 138, 157
Rushton Hall, Northamptonshire 96

Sackville, Lord John 119
Sackville, John Frederick 119
Sackville, Mortimer Sackville-West, 1st Baron 34
Sackville family 34
Sackville-West, Vita 41, 46–7, 90, 103
St Luke's Club of Artists 50
Sales, John 150
Salisbury, Lord 121
Selwyn, George 75
Shakespeare, William 10
Shaw, R Norman 133
Sheffield, Henry Holroyd, 3rd Earl of 122
Sheffield Park, East Sussex 122, 138, 139
Sherrif, George 131
Shrewsbury, Anna Brudenell, Countess of 60–61
Shrewsbury, Elizabeth Talbot, Countess of (Bess of Hardwick) 86–7, 118
Shrewsbury, Francis Talbot, 11th Earl of 60
Shrewsbury, George Talbot, 6th Earl of 86–7
Shugborough, Staffordshire 74
Simpson, John 97–8
Sissinghurst Castle Garden, Kent 41, 46–7, 103
Skinner, George Ure 128
Sleter, Francesco 69
sloth 108–123
Smith, Professor Sir William Wright 105
Snowshill Manor, Gloucestershire 20–22
Soames, Arthur 138, 139
Soames, Captain Granville 139
Society of Dilettanti 73–4
Society (or Knights) of St Francis of Wycombe 74

Somerset, Lady Anne 136
South Lodge, Sussex 138
Spencer, Lady Diana (Princess Diana) 81
Spenser, Edmund 69
Stalin, Joseph 112
Stanley House, London 65
Stevens, 'Lumpy' 119
Stoney-Bowes, Andrew Robinson 65
Stourhead, Wiltshire 47–8, 67
Stowe, Buckinghamshire 49–53, 73, 74, 76, 78, 123
Stowe Landscape Gardens, Buckinghamshire 68–71
Streeter, Fred 161
Stroud, Dorothy 52
Stuart, James 'Athenian' 74
Studley Royal Water Garden (& Fountains Abbey), North Yorkshire 97–8
Sutherland, George Sutherland-Leveson-Gower, 2nd Duke of 141, 142
Sutherland, Harriet, Duchess of 142
Sutton Courtenay, Oxfordshire 102
Switzer, Stephen 22, 82, 144

Tatton Park, Cheshire 99
Teleki, Count 63–4
Thackeray, William Makepeace 59, 59, 65
Theobalds Park, Hertfordshire 88
Thomas, Norman 159
Thoroton, Robert 62
Throckmorton, Muriel 96
Throckmorton, Sir Robert 110
Toland, John 52
Torrington, John 15
Trebah gardens, Cornwall 145
Trentham Hall, Stoke-on-Trent, Staffordshire 141, 142
Tresham, Francis 96
Tresham, Sir Thomas 88–9, 96
Tucker, John, MP 75
Turner, Roger 16–17
Turner, William (J M W Turner) 111

Upton House, Warwickshire 66

Vanbrugh, Sir John 50, 68, 85, 114
Vane-Tempest-Stewart, Lady Mairi
    (later Bury) 37, 38
Vansittart, Sir Henry 75
Veitch, James (father and son) 148
Veitch, John 147–8
Veitch nursery company 137
Victoria, Queen 32, 88, 114
Vincent, Victor 112

Waddesdon Manor,
    Buckinghamshire 101, 149–51
Wade, Charles Paget 20–22
Wakehurst Place, West Sussex 138
Walpole, Horace, 4th Earl of Orford
    22, 24, 31, 50, 51, 52, 71–4, 154
Walpole, Sir Robert 53, 97
Warrington, George Booth, 2nd Earl
    of 14, 15
Warwick, Frances, Countess of 149
Wesley, Rev. John 69, 72
West, Gilbert 68, 69
West Wycombe Park and
    Medmenham Abbey,
    Buckinghamshire 71–9, 73
Westbury Court, Gloucestershire
    54–5
Westminster, Hugh Lupus
    Grosvenor, 1st Duke of 155

Westmorland, John Fane, 10th Earl
    of 66
Whiteknights Park, Berkshire 151
Whitmore-Jones, Dorothy 42
Whitmore-Jones, John 42
Whitmore-Jones, Walter 113
Wilde, Oscar 59
Wilkes, John 75, 76, 78
William III, King (William of
    Orange) 54, 82, 147
Willis, George 144
Willis, Peter 50
Wimpole Hall, Cambridgeshire
    22–5
Windham, William, I 14
Windham, William, II 123
Wingfield, Major Walter C 121, 122
Winthrop, Gertrude 103, 104
Wise, Henry 81–2
Wodehouse, P G 106
Woolf, Leonard 90
Woolf, Virginia 90
wrath 100–107
Wrest Park, Bedfordshire 23
Wright, Orville 99
Wyatt, Lewis 99

Yorke, Agneta 93
Yorke family (at Erdigg) 33

zeal 124–39

Acknowledgements

The biggest 'Thanks!' are owed Margaret Willes who inaugurated
this book and worked with such enthusiasm and Samantha
Wyndham for all her burrowing through endless files and folders.
But most of all for their great humour and revealing where to find
the best Bloody Mary in London!

A big thanks to my great agent, Sarah Dalkin; and as always to
Terry & Tasso. Thanks also to Merlin Waterson and Richard
Bisgrove for permission to quote from their books.

Thanks also to all National Trust gardeners and staff who
provided so many great stories and helped make the book
happen; and to all at Anova Books.

And, of course, all the 'sinners' who created such wonderful
gardens which now provide so much enjoyment to garden
visitors and historians.